The Helpful Leader

The Helpful Leader

JAMES OYOLA

In Their Own Words...

"I had the pleasure of working with James for the better part of two years during my time at Centerfield Media (formerly, Qology Direct) when I served as the company's Chief Information Officer. We hired James as our Director of Quality Assurance, where he reported to me and helped build the company's QA team across our U.S., Jamaica, and South Africa locations. James is passionate, talented, and solution-driven. His biggest asset is his ability to not just mentor and coach others but also manage varying types of personnel issues in order to seek cohesion on his teams. I've seen James build a family-like culture with his team, which transitioned into production-driven results."

- Brian McLaughlin, Chief Technology Officer, EarthLink Internet

"James is a personable Servant Leader. He takes the time to understand the tasks he delegates to his team and follows through to assist if needed, and ensures completion on time. His leadership skills are focused on team and individual employee development," **- David Croxton, Retired Director of Privacy, CIPP/US, CIPT, CIPM, CISSP, CISA, CRISC**

"Working with James Oyola was one of the most impactful experiences of my career. In a fast-moving world of constant pressure, he led with clarity, confidence, and encouragement, making even the toughest goals feel achievable by rolling up his sleeves alongside us. What set him apart was his ability to inspire—his contagious energy, meaningful words, and habit of turning setbacks into learning moments built resilience and belief in ourselves. He didn't just focus on results; he focused on people. His leadership created an environment where people felt supported, challenged, and valued, fostering loyalty, pride, and a culture that continues to shape how I think about leadership today."

- Anna Singh, Senior Director, Customer Care Operations

 FWC26 Value:

Respectful, Owners & Flexible

James is a strong communicator, focuses on collaboration, shows empathy, and listens well. He is more than just a leader.

He's a mentor who truly understands people beyond words. His ability to read situations, offer insightful advice, and engage in meaningful conversations sets him apart.

He fosters an environment of trust, support, and growth, making every challenge feel manageable. His leadership is not just about guidance; it's about connection, wisdom, and inspiration. James always has positive energy, a calm demeanor, and a professional attitude that make him a pleasure to work with.

ABOUT MVP NOMINEE:
JAMES OYOLA

CONTENTS

Introduction

Montego Bay, Jamaica, 2017. 7:45 A.M.

The client was furious, and I had about 30 seconds to de-escalate a bad situation. I pushed through the office doors mid-sentence, phone pressed to my ear, nodding at my team with a quick wave as I beelined to my office.

Just need to solve this, I thought. *Then I can breathe.*

Two hours later, crisis averted, I emerged ready to debrief the team. That's when Keisha appeared at my door.

"Everything alright, James?"

I blinked. "Yeah, why? We just saved the account."

"It's just... You seemed upset this morning. The whole team thought something was wrong."

I replayed the morning. The rushed entry. The wave without words. The closed door.

"I wasn't upset," I said. "I was handling an emergency."

Keisha nodded slowly, choosing her words carefully. "In Jamaica, when you pass someone without a proper greeting, it signals something is wrong. We've all been worried that we upset you somehow. No one could focus."

I had saved the account. But I'd lost my team's trust in the same breath. Because I'd forgotten something essential: in many cultures, relationships aren't separate from work. They are the work. And leadership happens not in the big strategic wins, but in the small human moments we rush past without thinking.

That morning cost me nothing on the P&L, but it cost me something far more valuable: two hours of my team's focus, confidence, and sense of psychological safety. All because I didn't understand that a greeting isn't just a matter of politeness. It's how you tell people I see you. You matter. We're in this together.

I have worked in the corporate sector for the past 20 years, specifically in customer care, leading domestic and international teams. Business Process Outsourcing has been the focus of my career, with most of my time spent in senior leadership roles across three main functional areas: Training and Development, Quality Assurance, and Operations. I've had the pleasure of working with clients such as Walmart, Sprint Wireless, and The Home Depot. I also spent eight years as a national sports journalist.

In 2019, I received The Home Depot's "Building Strong Relationships" award, which validated something I'd always believed: even organizations generating over $150 billion in annual revenue (2024) understand that relationships, not just results, drive sustainable success. That award marked the first time a company formally acknowledged the additional steps I was taking to truly care for its people, and it reinforced that values-aligned leadership resonates at every organizational level.

I currently work in the Customer Care department of one of the world's largest sports organizations. One of the greatest privileges in working for a company of this size is the ability to work closely with people from every corner of the earth. When it comes to working in diverse environments, my time here takes the cake.

Every day, I receive confirmation of what I have concluded throughout my career: At the end of the day, no matter where someone is from, people thrive on feeling seen, appreciated, and valued, and on working with others who support them.

My experiences have both fortified and challenged my ability to communicate effectively.

See, it's not until one shares space and time with people from other parts of the world that they understand the true beauty and complexity of effective communication. It's an art that ignites collaboration and innovation by bringing diverse perspectives and ideas together. Working in a setting where global perspectives converge cultivates unparalleled personal and professional growth, as every interaction challenges you to think beyond your own cultural lens. Daily exposure to multiple languages and diverse beliefs builds emotional intelligence and adaptability, empowering you to communicate and collaborate with empathy and confidence. When differences are embraced as strengths, the result is a dynamic environment that accelerates mental resilience, creativity, and leadership skills in ways few experiences can match.

The Evolution of Leadership

Leadership has evolved dramatically over the past century, shaped by economic conditions, technological advancement, and shifting cultural values. While this evolution followed distinct trajectories across regions, certain patterns emerged universally, reflecting a global shift from authoritarian command-and-control toward collaborative, purpose-driven leadership.

In Europe, leadership theories progressed from the 'Great Men' concept of inherent traits in the early 1900s through behavioral approaches emphasizing what leaders do at mid-century, to contingency models recognizing that effective leadership depends on situational context by the 1960s-70s, culminating in transformational theories focusing on inspiring change and vision in the 1980s-90s. The tumultuous 20th century, marked by world wars, depression, and social upheaval, gave rise to inclusive leadership models across Europe and other developed nations. These international perspectives, including significant scholarly contributions from institutions such as Oxford University, enriched the global conversation about what constitutes effective leadership, demonstrating that while cultural contexts differ, the fundamental evolution transcends borders.

In the United States, the Silent Generation (1925-1945) and Baby Boomers (1946-1964) built their careers during eras of economic expansion and organizational stability, leading them to embrace hierarchy-driven leadership where loyalty to the organization was paramount. During this period, women leaders like Eleanor Roosevelt redefined what leadership could look like, becoming influential advocates for civil rights, women's rights, and human rights during Franklin D. Roosevelt's presidency and later playing a crucial role in drafting the Universal Declaration of Human Rights. By mid-century, pioneering leaders like Indira Gandhi, the first and only female Prime Minister of India, and Margaret Thatcher, the United Kingdom's first female Prime Minister who held office from 1979 to 1990, demonstrated that women could lead nations through economic transformation and global crisis.

However, Generation X (1965-1980) entered the workforce during economic recessions, corporate downsizing, and the collapse of the "lifetime employment" promise, which bred skepticism toward institutions and shifted leadership thinking toward competence-based models. These leaders value independence, results over hours worked, and work-life balance, creating their own career security rather than depending on organizational loyalty.

This generational experience fundamentally changed what leadership meant, shifting it from "climb the ladder and stay loyal" to "prove your value and adapt or die."

Generation X also witnessed a pivotal demographic shift: they were the first generation to see a substantial rise in dual-income households as women entered the workforce in large numbers during the 1980s. The women's suffrage movements of the 19th and 20th centuries turned Enlightenment ideals into action, with milestones such as the 19th Amendment in the U.S. in 1920 and women's suffrage victories in the UK in 1918 and 1928 laying the groundwork. Now, Gen X saw those earlier victories translate into women breaking through corporate glass ceilings at unprecedented rates, challenging the male-dominated executive landscape that had defined previous generations.

Millennials (1981-1999) further transformed leadership by prioritizing collaboration, purpose, and continuous feedback, a shift driven by their upbringing during rapid technological change, the 2008 financial crisis, and exposure to global connectivity. Where previous generations saw leadership as positional authority earned through seniority, Millennials view leadership as "pulling together" with peers toward shared goals, valuing open communication, immediate results, and meaningful work over traditional hierarchy.

Technology accelerated this change: constant connectivity replaced formal memos, collaborative digital tools replaced rigid chains of command, and transparency became an expectation rather than a courtesy.

The Millennial generation also accelerated women's representation in leadership positions. Women are more ambitious than ever: 9 out of 10 women ages 30 and under want to be promoted to the next level, and 3 out of 4 aspire to senior leadership roles. Figures like Ellen Johnson Sirleaf, who became Africa's first democratically elected female head of state in 2005 and won the Nobel Peace Prize in 2011 for her work promoting peace and women's rights, and Jacinda Ardern, who became New Zealand's youngest prime minister in 2017 at age 37 and earned international acclaim for her compassionate leadership during crises like the Christchurch Mosque attacks and COVID-19 pandemic, exemplified this shift. This generation normalized the expectation that women would occupy C-suite positions and boardrooms, not as exceptions, but as the standard.

Generation Z (2000–2012) is now amplifying this evolution. Raised in a fully digital world and shaped by social media, global movements, and economic uncertainty, Gen Z expects leaders to be authentic, socially responsible, and inclusive. They value diversity, mental health, and flexibility as much as compensation. For this generation, diversity matters across multiple dimensions, not just race and gender, but also identity, orientation, and background, and they expect companies to better represent this spectrum of differences in both external branding and talent pipelines. With women now making up 47% of the workforce, Gen Z doesn't view women in leadership as exceptional. They view it as the baseline expectation.

Generation Alpha (2013 onward) will push leadership into uncharted territory. Growing up in an era of AI, automation, and immersive technology, they will expect hyper-personalized experiences, instant access to information, and seamless integration of work and life. The result is a modern leadership landscape where effectiveness is measured not by title or tenure, but by the ability to inspire, adapt, communicate across platforms, and create environments where diverse skills and perspectives unite toward collective success.

Today's leaders must balance the discipline and loyalty of earlier generations with the agility, inclusivity, and purpose-driven approach demanded by the modern workforce. The journey from suffrage to board seats, from Michelle Bachelet to Wangari Maathai and countless female CEOs, illustrates that the rise of women in leadership has been one of the most transformative forces in reshaping what leadership looks and sounds like, bringing empathy, collaboration, and authentic vulnerability into spaces that once valued only stoicism and dominance.

In today's workforce, the beacon of success has shifted from profit and loss to employee morale and engagement. Organizations are realizing that a motivated and fulfilled team drives innovation, customer satisfaction, and long-term sustainability far more effectively than short-term financial gains. High morale fosters collaboration and resilience, while engagement ensures employees are invested in the company's mission, creating a culture where success is measured not just by numbers, but by the strength and loyalty of its people.

The Three Pillars of Effective Leadership

One way organizations can achieve this is by hiring and developing effective leaders. Leadership, at its core, is the ability to inspire, influence, and guide others toward shared goals, fostering personal growth and organizational success. While some individuals may possess natural traits, charisma, confidence, or decisiveness that give them an initial advantage, these innate qualities alone do not guarantee effective leadership. True leadership effectiveness results from intentional development, continuous learning, and the ability to adapt to complex human dynamics. In other words, while some people may be "born leaders" in terms of personality or presence, effective leaders are made through the deliberate cultivation of skills, emotional intelligence, and adaptive strategies that address real-world challenges. John Wooden once said, *"Talent will get you to the top, but it takes character to keep you there."*

Companies that aspire to cultivate effective leaders should focus their development efforts on three core areas: Emotional Intelligence, Effective Communication, and Conflict Resolution.

Emotional Intelligence

Throughout the last century of evolving leadership principles, the term Emotional Intelligence first appeared in 1985 in Wayne Payne's doctoral thesis, "A Study of Emotion: Developing Emotional Intelligence." His thesis highlighted that emotional awareness and regulation are critical for personal well-being and social harmony, challenging the long-standing notion that emotions should be suppressed. This idea laid out the foundation for later research, most notably Daniel Goleman's work, which showed that EI (also known as EQ) is essential for leadership, teamwork, and mental health. As a result, organizations, educators, and mental health professionals began integrating emotional intelligence into training, creating healthier workplaces, and improving interpersonal relationships globally.

In his book, "Working with Emotional Intelligence," Goleman proposed that, "We are being judged by a new yardstick; not just how smart we are, or by our training and expertise, but also how well we handle ourselves and each other."

Shoshana Zuboff, a former social psychologist and retired professor at Harvard Business School, was quoted in another book of Goleman's, saying that "Corporations have gone through a radical revolution within this century, and with this has come a corresponding transformation of the emotional landscape. There was a long period of managerial domination of the corporate hierarchy, during which the manipulative, jungle-fighter boss was rewarded. But that rigid hierarchy began to break down in the 1980s under the twin pressures of globalization and information technology. The jungle fighter symbolizes where corporations have been; the virtuoso in interpersonal skills is the corporate future."

This shift reflects a fundamental change in what organizations value: collaboration and adaptability have replaced rigid control as the keys to success. Globalization and technology have created interconnected workplaces where emotional intelligence and interpersonal skills are essential for managing diverse teams and rapid change. Today, leaders who inspire trust, communicate effectively, and build relationships are seen as the true drivers of corporate growth, signaling a future in which empathy and agility outweigh dominance and manipulation.

Effective Communication

As the laborer increases in EQ, this level of self-awareness will help them identify how their communication is, or isn't, conducive to achieving the overall business goals. Effective Communication is another core trait for strong leaders. **From a purely financial standpoint, organizations with highly effective communicators see measurable returns:** companies with strong communication practices are 3.5 times more likely to outperform their peers, and poor communication costs businesses an average of $62.4 million annually in lost productivity. Investing in communication skills isn't just good for morale; it's a direct driver of profitability and competitive advantage.

When teams share knowledge across borders, they create more creative and inclusive solutions. Strong communication also builds trust and strengthens relationships, ensuring alignment across cultures and time zones, an essential factor for multinational projects. Cultural intelligence is key in this space and helps teams adapt quickly to changing environments and market demands.

Conflict Resolution

Rounding out the last pillar of what makes an effective leader is Conflict Resolution. Conflict is inevitable in all interpersonal relationships because differences in perspectives, values, and communication styles are natural. In the workplace, these differences often surface during decision-making, collaboration, or resource allocation. Rather than viewing conflict as a threat, effective leaders recognize it as an opportunity for growth, innovation, and stronger relationships. When managed constructively, conflict can lead to better problem-solving and deeper understanding among team members, ultimately improving organizational performance.

However, unresolved or poorly handled conflict can damage trust, lower morale, and hinder productivity. This is why leaders must develop skills in active listening, empathy, and negotiation to turn disagreements into progress. As Thomas Crum, a renowned expert in conflict resolution, states, "The quality of our lives depends not on whether or not we have conflicts, but on how we respond to them." This perspective underscores that the driver of success for an effective leader is not avoiding conflict but responding to it with clarity, fairness, and emotional intelligence.

See, leading effectively is not about positional authority or a title; it is the intentional practice of serving, elevating, and empowering those entrusted to your care. This approach produces organizations marked by higher engagement, stronger retention, and sustainable success that extends far beyond any single leader's tenure.

The Helpful Leader Framework

Applying principles taught in the help profession space is essential for a leader to make lasting change in the workplace. A help professional is someone whose primary role is to assist individuals in improving their well-being, coping with challenges, or achieving personal and professional goals. This term often refers to people in fields like counseling, social work, psychology, healthcare, and coaching; professions centered on providing guidance, support, and resources to others. Their work typically involves empathy, problem-solving, and ethical responsibility to promote positive outcomes for those they serve.

These qualities translate directly into effective leadership in the workplace. Leaders who demonstrate empathy can understand and address their team's needs. Strong problem-solving skills enable them to navigate challenges with clarity and confidence, ensuring that decisions benefit both individuals and the organization. Ethical responsibility ensures fairness and integrity, which are essential for building credibility and maintaining a positive work culture.

By applying these principles, leaders create an environment where employees feel valued and supported, driving engagement and long-term success.

Regardless of perspective, effective leaders embody the principles of servant leadership. They represent the essence of the inverted pyramid, in which the individual at the highest rank serves as the anchor and support for the entire organization. This approach prioritizes empowering others, fostering collaboration, and ensuring that the team's success comes before personal gain. By serving rather than commanding, effective leaders create a culture of trust and accountability that drives sustainable results.

"The Helpful Leader" is built on the belief that leadership is not about authority, but about service and support. By applying the principles of helping professions, empathy, problem-solving, and ethical responsibility, leaders can create workplaces where people thrive, and organizations achieve lasting success.

What to Expect

Throughout our time together, I will attempt to dive deeper into these three core areas and the foundational qualities of the helping professions. Through pithy statements, personal experiences, quotes, and aphorisms, I aim to unpack what it means to steward your leadership role well. In one way, shape, or form, we will all be in the "people business" throughout the entirety of our lives. In essence, becoming an expert in humanity is not just a growth strategy; it is the foundation for sustainable leadership and organizational success. I don't expect you to become an expert by the time you finish this book, but I do hope to plant seeds in the good soil of your heart, seeds that will grow and bear abundant fruit in your workplace.

Chapter 1:

Understanding the Leader in You

Exceptional leaders possess a clear understanding of who they are. Their sense of identity shapes how they view themselves in the leadership role and influences every interaction with their team. This self-knowledge goes beyond surface-level awareness; it encompasses a deep familiarity with their cognitive strengths, emotional patterns, social capabilities, and the unique contexts in which they operate best. They recognize their natural abilities and acknowledge where growth is needed. Aware of the pressures and constraints they face, effective leaders can guide from the front when necessary or support from behind when appropriate. They understand their knowledge gaps and the boundaries of their influence, which drives them toward continuous personal development. Rather than imposing their vision on others, they intentionally create environments where people genuinely want to participate and contribute.

Effective leaders also possess keen insight into the people they serve. Their constituencies are diverse, ranging from employees and stakeholders to community members at local, national, and global levels. A leader's capacity to create impact hinges on whether those they serve view them as credible and trustworthy. People's willingness to be influenced largely depends on how authentically the leader engages with them and how skillfully they shape behavior through meaningful connection. It's been said before that, "You have to be in it to win it." Through intentional relationship-building, active presence, and adaptive communication strategies, leaders demonstrate credibility and earn the trust necessary for genuine influence.

Authentic leadership begins with the understanding that authenticity is not something a leader can simply claim for themselves. As noted in the Harvard Business Review article Managing Authenticity: The Paradox of Great Leadership, "Authenticity is a quality that others must attribute to you. No leader can look into a mirror and say, 'I am authentic.'" This perspective underscores that authenticity is earned through behavior, not self-proclamation.

To lead authentically is to be genuine, an individual rather than an imitation. Authentic leaders have a strong sense of self, and others trust them because their actions consistently reflect their values. They share openly to build trust, recognizing that shared goals rely on that foundation. They also understand the importance of support systems and rely on teams to help them achieve meaningful outcomes.

Authentic leaders invite diverse viewpoints, remain accessible across all levels of the organization, and leverage technology to strengthen communication. They cultivate transparency by acknowledging mistakes publicly and explaining the reasoning behind their decisions. In doing so, they create an environment where trust, clarity, and collaboration can thrive.

How effectively a leader frames situations and interactions directly impacts their ability to achieve meaningful outcomes. Leaders who excel at crafting narratives, who understand how to tell compelling stories that resonate emotionally, build deeper and more enduring connections with their teams. Storytelling isn't simply about sharing information; it's about creating shared meaning, inspiring action, and helping people see themselves as part of something larger. When leaders communicate with authenticity and purpose, they don't just convey facts; they shape how people interpret reality, respond to challenges, and envision possibilities. This ability to frame experiences and articulate a vision transforms a competent manager into a transformational leader who moves hearts, not just metrics.

Understanding who you are as a leader and recognizing the people you serve establishes the foundation. But that foundation alone doesn't build the structure. The principles we've explored in this chapter, self-awareness, people's intelligence, and the power of narrative, must be translated into daily practice. Leadership isn't theoretical; it's lived out in the thousands of micro decisions, interactions, and moments that make up your day.

How do you respond when someone on your team makes a costly mistake? What do you do when two high performers are in conflict? How do you balance the competing demands of organizational goals and individual needs? These are the questions that separate leaders who understand the concept from leaders who embody the practice.

In the chapters that follow, you'll find specific leadership rules designed to help you navigate the complex realities of leading people. These aren't abstract ideals; they are practical guidelines forged from real experience in diverse workplaces. Some will challenge your assumptions. Others will validate instincts you've had but couldn't quite articulate. I've heard it said that "common sense isn't always common practice." Each rule is an invitation to examine your current approach and consider whether adjustments might better serve both your team and your organization.

One of my mentors, Nestor Medina, shared something his mentor taught him, and it stayed with me throughout my career.

"Repetition is the key to learning, retaining, and confidence."

This truth transforms how we approach leadership development. Becoming an effective leader requires practice, and every single day at the office is an opportunity to grow in this area. Each interaction with your team, every difficult conversation, and each moment you choose empathy over impatience are repetitions in the discipline of leadership. If you view each day through this lens, as a chance to build one step closer toward becoming a leader who genuinely cares, you'll find that growth compounds over time through consistent repetition.

We're always building in one direction or another. Toward the leader we aspire to be or away from it. There is no neutral. The question isn't whether you'll practice leadership today; it's whether you'll practice it intentionally, knowing that repetition is what turns knowledge into skill, skill into habit, and habit into character. The principles in this book aren't meant to be read once and shelved. They're meant to be practiced repeatedly until they become part of your identity as a leader.

Chapter 2:

The Foundation of Leadership

Leadership Rule #19 - "There is no point in focusing on structure without a foundation to support it…"

Effective leaders would do well to recognize that true strength lies not in the visible structure but in the invisible foundation. Before erecting the edifice of success, they diligently craft the underlying framework that sustains it. Let us prioritize the patient work of building foundations, for it is upon this solid ground that our most ambitious structures will rise.

Think of it like playing a video game: Before you can take on the final boss or build the coolest gear, you must grind through the early levels, collect resources, and level up your character. That behind-the-scenes work isn't flashy, but it's what makes you strong enough to handle the big challenges later.

Leadership works the same way. Laying down the groundwork is like leveling up your stats, so when the real test comes, you're ready to win.

Throughout my career, I've witnessed countless leaders chase visible wins while neglecting the invisible work that sustains them. They focus on metrics, KPIs, and quarterly results, the structure, while overlooking the foundational investment in their people. They want the scoreboard to reflect success without understanding that the game is won in practice, not during the performance.

The most effective leaders I've encountered understood a simple truth: You cannot build trust on Tuesday and expect loyalty on Wednesday. You cannot skip the developmental work of emotional intelligence, effective communication, and conflict resolution, and then wonder why your team crumbles under pressure.

This principle echoes throughout the helping professions (counseling, social work, and psychology fields we discussed in the Introduction), where practitioners know that sustainable change never happens at the surface level. A therapist doesn't just address symptoms; they work through root causes. A social worker doesn't simply provide immediate relief; they build systems of support that endure the crisis. Similarly, leaders who rush to implement new processes, reorganize teams, or launch initiatives without first establishing a foundation of trust, clarity, and shared values are building on sand. The first storm, whether it's a difficult client, an organizational shift, or interpersonal conflict, will reveal what's missing beneath.

As I've worked alongside people from many parts of the world, I've learned that this truth transcends culture, language, and industry. People don't thrive under leaders who prioritize optics over integrity, or speed over sustainability. They thrive when they know their leader has done the patient, quiet work of becoming someone worth following, not because of their title, but because of their character.

Leadership Rule #3 - "A good steward of the now, becomes a great teacher of tomorrow, and ends up an excellent elder who leads by example..."

In the delicate balance between caution and anxiety, faith serves as the anchor, allowing us to navigate the unknown with discerning eyes, prepared for the unexpected yet unshackled from the weight of fear and doubt.

Good stewardship of the present moment requires embracing the sacred balance between trust and prudence, hope and humility, and faith and foresight, and acknowledging that the art of living well is not in controlling the future but in tenderly cultivating the soil of the present, where love, wisdom, and growth flourish.

In simpler terms, living wisely is like tending to a small garden. You don't control the weather, but you can water the plants, pull the weeds, and give them sunlight. The care you give today shapes what grows tomorrow. Just as a gardener must trust that seeds will sprout if nurtured, we can focus on the actions within our reach, such as patience, kindness, and effort, knowing that these small choices build strength for whatever comes next.

Often, I've observed patterns that distinguish those who merely occupy leadership positions from those who genuinely shape those around them. The difference isn't found in their strategic vision or operational brilliance. **It's found in how they handle the mundane moments.** The difficult conversation with an underperforming team member, the choice to listen when it would be easier to dictate, the decision to invest time in someone's development when deadlines are screaming. These present-moment choices, repeated consistently, become the invisible curriculum that teaches those around you what leadership looks like. The leader who rushes past these moments in pursuit of tomorrow's results forfeits the very influence they hope to build.

This principle mirrors what we see across professions where mastery is built through present-moment dedication. A surgeon doesn't defer the meticulous work of suturing (stitching up a wound or incision using surgical thread) to "when there's less pressure." An educator doesn't postpone challenging conversations with a struggling student until the semester is less chaotic. A firefighter doesn't wait for ideal conditions before entering a burning building. They steward the now, the precise movement, the difficult question, the calculated risk, because they understand that excellence is forged in the crucible of the present, not in the comfort of tomorrow's promise.

Leaders who embrace this same posture create environments where people feel genuinely seen and valued, not as future assets, but as human beings worthy of attention right now.

Working alongside colleagues from every continent has reinforced this truth for me. Regardless of language, culture, or background, people instinctively recognize when a leader is fully present with them versus when they're merely transacting business.

That recognition becomes the foundation of trust, and trust is the currency that transforms positional authority into genuine influence. The kind that inspires people to follow you, not because they must, but because they want to. But you don't earn that trust by chasing tomorrow's wins; you earn it by faithfully stewarding the interactions, conversations, and relationships that exist right in front of you today.

Indra Nooyi (former CEO of PepsiCo) once said that *"Leadership is hard to define, and good leadership is even harder. But if you can get people to follow you to the ends of the earth, you are a great leader."*

Chapter 3:

Self-Awareness and Personal Growth

Leadership Rule #22 - "The best inspection is introspection..."

As we strive to become effective leaders, we must courageously examine our own biases, strengths, and weaknesses. Through introspective leadership, we foster a culture of self-awareness, accountability, and continuous improvement (see Kaizen).

In doing so, we can accomplish the following:

- Enhanced self-awareness
- Improved decision-making
- Increased empathy
- Better stress management

This approach can yield a positive return on investment (ROI) for companies because when leaders practice introspection, they set the tone for a culture built on honesty, learning, and adaptability. By examining biases, strengths, and weaknesses, leaders reduce blind spots and make better decisions. Self-awareness fosters accountability, thereby building trust across teams. Continuous improvement, as emphasized in the Japanese term "Kaizen," ensures that small, steady changes compound into long-term progress.

Together, these habits create an environment where employees feel empowered to contribute ideas, adapt to challenges, and align their efforts with organizational goals, ultimately driving sustainable success and desired results.

Toyota, founded in Japan, implemented Kaizen as a formal system in 1951 through its "Creative Idea Suggestion System," which has since generated billions of dollars in value and remains one of the world's longest-running employee innovation programs. Leaders at Toyota consistently examine processes, identify inefficiencies, and encourage employees at every level to contribute ideas for improvement. This introspective approach, which acknowledges strengths, weaknesses, and biases, has enabled Toyota to build a culture of accountability, innovation, and resilience.

Brene Brown once said, *"Owning our story can be hard, but not nearly as difficult as spending our lives running from it. Embracing our vulnerabilities is risky but not nearly as dangerous as giving up on love and belonging and joy, the experiences that make us the most vulnerable. Only when we are brave enough to explore the darkness will we discover the infinite power of our light."*

Leadership Rule #49 - "A strong work ethic is necessary, but must go through constant safety inspections..."

A strong work ethic is the backbone of any successful individual. It's the driving force that pushes us to strive for excellence, to innovate, and to make a meaningful impact. However, it's equally important to recognize that our work ethic is often shaped by our past experiences and motivations.

As leaders, it's crucial that we take the time to reflect on the underlying drivers of our work ethic. Are we driven by a genuine passion for our work, or are we motivated by external factors such as validation or competition? Understanding the roots of our work ethic can help us build a healthier and more sustainable foundation for success.

I've personally witnessed the double-edged sword of a relentless work ethic. I've seen leaders burn themselves out chasing metrics that feed their ego rather than their purpose. I've watched talented professionals sacrifice their health, relationships, and mental well-being on the altar of productivity, only to discover that what they built crumbled the moment they stepped away. The question isn't whether you work hard, it's why you work hard and at what cost.

Here's the challenge: Most of us don't know what's fueling our drive. We tell ourselves it's passion, commitment, or responsibility, and those things may be part of it, but beneath the surface, insecurity, unresolved trauma, or the need to prove our worth often quietly steer the ship. These

13

hidden motivations don't announce themselves; they disguise themselves as dedication. A work ethic fueled by these unexamined drivers will eventually corrode the very success it produces.

Without regular self-examination, what appears to be dedication can quietly morph into dysfunction, and what looks like strength can mask an unwillingness to rest, delegate, or trust others.

The difficulty is that we rarely see it in ourselves. We only recognize the symptoms: chronic exhaustion, strained relationships, or the quiet sense that no accomplishment ever feels like enough.

Think of it like maintaining an aircraft. A plane engine is built for power and endurance; it's designed to carry people across continents and through turbulent skies. But even the most powerful engine requires scheduled inspections, routine maintenance, and mandatory downtimes. Pilots don't question whether the engine can keep running; they ask whether it should keep running without checking for stress fractures, worn components, or compromised systems. Ignoring these safety protocols doesn't demonstrate strength; it guarantees catastrophic failure at altitude. Similarly, leaders who refuse to inspect the emotional and psychological infrastructure behind their work ethic aren't demonstrating commitment; they're courting collapse. The strongest leaders aren't those who never rest; they're the ones who recognize that sustainable excellence requires honest assessment of what's driving them, intentional rhythms of renewal, and the humility to admit when their "engine" needs attention before it fails mid-flight.

Here are three action steps to help you cultivate a healthy work ethic:

1. **Reflect on your motivations**: Take time to reflect on what drives your work ethic. Ask yourself whether your motivations align with your values and passions. We all have blind spots; we all need to invest in seeing them.

2. **Focus on intrinsic rewards**: Instead of relying on external validation or rewards, focus on the intrinsic satisfaction and fulfillment that come from doing meaningful work.

3. **Prioritize self-care**: Recognize that a healthy work ethic is not just about productivity, but also about taking care of your physical, emotional, and mental well-being. Make time for rest, relaxation, and activities that nourish your mind, body, and spirit. The best thing about a strong work ethic is how contagious it can be. But no one will want to emulate a burned-out, bitter achiever.

We'll explore this 'below the surface' dynamic more fully in Chapter 21 with the Iceberg Model of Leadership.

Chapter 4:

Mental and Emotional Well-being

Leadership Rule #111 - "It's ok to not be ok..."

Burnout is real. If you're not careful, your work ethic can lead to your demise. Part of being an effective leader is being reliable, and we can't be reliable if we are not ok. When leaders acknowledge they're struggling, they model strength through vulnerability and create space for others to do the same. Recognizing when your emotional or mental tank is empty is not only responsible; it's essential for sustainable leadership. Asking for help is not a detour from leadership; it's a direct path to resilience and growth.

Think about how caffeine works. Most people believe coffee gives them energy, but that's not what's happening at the neurological level. Throughout the day, a chemical called adenosine builds up in your brain. It's the body's natural signal that you're tired and need rest. Caffeine doesn't make you less tired; it simply blocks the adenosine receptors, preventing you from feeling the tiredness that's still accumulating beneath the surface.

This is why the caffeine crash feels so brutal: when the caffeine wears off, all that unaddressed tiredness hits you at once. You weren't actually rested. You were just biochemically prevented from receiving the signal that you needed rest.

Many leaders operate the same way. They use busyness, ambition, perfectionism, or sheer willpower to block the internal signals telling them they're depleted, hurting, or operating unsustainably. They caffeinate their way through exhaustion, not with literal coffee, but with performance, validation-seeking, or constant activity. The problem is, just as with adenosine, the exhaustion doesn't go away because you've blocked the signal. It accumulates. And when the crash comes, and it always comes, it's devastating.

For decades, the corporate world celebrated leaders who operated like machines, tireless, emotionless, always available, perpetually "on."

Generation X and Baby Boomers built their careers in environments where admitting struggle was equated with incompetence, where vulnerability was perceived as liability, and where the unspoken rule was simple: Keep going no matter what.

But as Millennials and Gen Z have entered leadership ranks, bringing heightened awareness of mental health and work-life integration, the conversation has shifted.

What previous generations masked as "toughness" is now being recognized for what it often was: Unsustainable self-sacrifice that damaged leaders, their families, and ultimately their teams.

Today's workforce, informed by global connectivity, social movements around mental health, and increased awareness of trauma, expects leaders to be human, not superhuman. They expect authenticity over performance, presence over perfection.

The challenge is that many leaders still carry the internal scripts of earlier eras. Even when they intellectually embrace the idea that "it's ok to not be ok," their actions reveal a deeper belief that admitting struggle is a professional risk. They fear being perceived as weak, unreliable, or unfit for their role.

Yet research consistently shows the opposite: Leaders who acknowledge their limitations, seek support, and model healthy boundaries are more trusted, more effective, and better able to sustain long-term impact.

In 2012, neuroscientists at the University of Rochester discovered a remarkable finding. The brain has its own waste removal system, the glymphatic system, which operates almost exclusively during sleep. While you're awake, your brain cells are tightly packed, constantly processing information, solving problems, managing emotions, and making decisions. This neural activity produces metabolic waste, beta-amyloid proteins, tau proteins, and other neurotoxins that accumulate throughout the day like trash in an office building. But when you sleep, something extraordinary occurs: your brain cells shrink by about 60%, creating space between them, and cerebrospinal fluid floods through these expanded channels, flushing out the accumulated waste. This detoxification process happens 10-20 times more efficiently during deep sleep than when you're awake. Sleep isn't passive downtime; it's active maintenance, and without it, toxic waste builds up, leading to cognitive decline, emotional dysregulation, poor decision-making, and eventually neurodegenerative disease.

Leaders operate under the same principle. During waking hours, you're processing information, navigating conflict, making decisions, managing emotions, and absorbing the stress of organizational life, activities that produce psychological and emotional waste: unresolved tensions, accumulated frustrations, vicarious trauma from your team's struggles, and the weight of decisions that impacted people's lives. If you never create space to flush this accumulation out, you become cognitively foggy, emotionally reactive, relationally brittle, and spiritually depleted. Just as your brain requires sleep to maintain cognitive health, your soul requires intentional rest, Sabbath, reflection, silence, play, disconnection from work, to maintain emotional and spiritual health. Leaders who pride themselves on "never stopping," who wear exhaustion as a badge of honor, or who equate busyness with importance are, in effect, preventing their own glymphatic system from functioning. The toxins don't disappear just because you ignore them. They accumulate until they compromise your ability to lead effectively.

Arianna Huffington, founder of Thrive Global and former co-founder of The Huffington Post, captured this truth perfectly: "We think, mistakenly, that success is the result of the amount of time we put in at work, instead of the quality of time we put in." After literally passing out from exhaustion and breaking her cheekbone on her desk, she became a vocal advocate for redefining success beyond relentless hustle.

Her words reflect a profound truth: Effectiveness is not a function of endurance but of intentionality, self-awareness, and the courage to admit when we need to step back, recharge, or ask for help.

This principle aligns with what the helping professions have always known: You cannot pour from an empty cup.

Therapists are trained to monitor their own mental health, recognizing that unprocessed stress and vicarious trauma compromise their ability to serve clients effectively. Physicians are increasingly encouraged to seek peer support and mental health resources, understanding that their well-being directly impacts patient care. Educators are taught that self-care is not selfish; it's foundational to show up fully for students. Leaders must adopt the same posture.

Your brain and your soul cannot sustain quality output without regular detoxification. The leader who refuses to rest doesn't demonstrate strength; they guarantee their own cognitive and emotional decline. Rest isn't optional for leaders who want longevity. Strategic maintenance flushes out toxins so you can lead with clarity, wisdom, and emotional stability tomorrow. Without this intentional detoxification, you're not avoiding burnout; you're guaranteeing it.

Admitting that you are struggling is not an admission of failure; it's an act of stewardship. It protects your team from the collateral damage of unexamined exhaustion, prevents poor decision-making rooted in depletion, and creates a culture in which people feel empowered to be honest about their own struggles. In my own journey across customer care environments, high-pressure client relationships, and the intensity of coordinating a global event, I've learned that the leaders who endure are not the ones who never falter. They're the ones who recognize when they're faltering and have the humility to recalibrate before they break.

Three ways to bring awareness:

1.   **Practice Reflective Check-Ins:** Set aside time weekly to assess your emotional and mental well-being.

2.   **Normalize Vulnerability in Team Culture:** Share moments of personal challenge with your team (appropriately) and encourage open dialogue about mental health and support systems.

3.   **Build a Support Network**: Identify trusted peers, mentors, or professionals you can turn to for help. Make

reaching out a regular part of your leadership practice, not just a last resort.

One of the most challenging tensions a leader faces is how to rest authentically while remaining responsible for their teams.

Whenever I take a vacation away from work, I've developed a principle that guides this balance: "I might not always be available, but I am never inaccessible."

These two concepts, availability and accessibility, are distinct, and understanding the difference is essential for sustainable leadership.

Availability means being present, responsive, and actively engaged in your team's day-to-day operations. It means being in the workflow, answering questions, providing guidance, and staying in sync with the rhythm of work. Accessibility, however, speaks to something deeper: the assurance that, in moments of genuine crisis or critical need, your team knows they can reach you. This distinction protects both your well-being and your team's security.

Taking time away to rest, recharge, and invest in your personal life isn't a luxury; it's a necessity that directly impacts your long-term effectiveness. Burnout doesn't serve anyone. However, during that time, accessibility recognizes that leadership carries a weight of responsibility that doesn't disappear simply because you're on vacation. This isn't about checking emails from the beach or attending Zoom meetings during family dinners. It's ensuring that if something truly urgent arises, a crisis that requires your specific authority, a decision only you can make, or a situation where your absence would create genuine harm, your team has a pathway to reach you.

This approach requires discernment, trust, and clear boundaries. You must trust your leadership team to handle most issues without involving you. You must empower them to make decisions in your absence, developing their capacity to lead when you're not there. You must clearly communicate what constitutes a true emergency and what can wait until your return. When this balance is well struck, you model healthy boundaries while simultaneously demonstrating that your commitment to your team's success doesn't waver when you step away. You're teaching them that rest is sacred, but so is stewardship, and effective leaders honor both.

But acknowledging a struggle is only the first step. Leaders must then create practical frameworks that help people manage their reality while maintaining accountability. The outdated "leave your problems at the door" approach forces people to deny their humanity. The helpful leader instead offers tools, like the mental locker concept we'll explore in Chapter 9, that honor both the person's struggle and the team's need for focus.

Admitting "it's ok to not be ok" isn't weakness; it's wisdom. It's choosing to listen to the signal rather than block it. It addresses the underlying fatigue rather than merely masking it. Leaders who ignore their own adenosine, their soul's signal that something needs attention, don't avoid burnout; they guarantee it. The only question is whether you'll address it proactively through rest, reflection, and soul care, or whether you'll wait for the crash that forces you to address it reactively.

Leadership Rule # 26 - "The only thing we control is how we respond to what we can't control…"

As leaders, emotional regulation is crucial for effective decision-making, communication, and team management. Research shows that 77% of employees experience work-related stress, which can impact productivity and morale (American Psychological Association). By developing emotional intelligence, leaders can better navigate complex situations, build stronger relationships, and create a more positive work environment.

Think of a basketball point guard in the final minutes of a close game. The crowd is loud, the pressure is immense, and every decision matters. If the point guard allows frustration or panic to take over, they might rush a pass, force a poor shot, or lose focus on the play. But the great ones, like Magic Johnson or Chris Paul, regulate their emotions. They stay calm, read the defense, and make smart choices that elevate the whole team. Their composure under stress doesn't mean they ignore emotions; it means they channel them productively to keep everyone aligned and confident.

Leadership works the same way.

When leaders manage their emotions, they become the steady hand guiding the team through high-pressure situations. Just as athletes know that mental discipline is as important as physical skill, leaders who practice emotional regulation create resilience, trust, and consistent performance across the organization.

Emotional regulation is not about suppressing emotions, but about welcoming, understanding, and managing them in ways that promote well-being and success. Studies have found that employees who work for emotionally intelligent leaders are more likely to be engaged, motivated, and committed to their work (Hay Group). The Hay Group's work demonstrates that emotional intelligence isn't just a "soft skill." It's a measurable driver of organizational success. By embracing their emotions and developing emotional regulation skills, leaders can unlock their full potential, build stronger teams, and achieve greater success. Let's take the first step towards emotional awareness and growth.

Jacinda Ardern once said that *"One of the criticisms I've faced over the years is that I'm not aggressive enough or assertive enough, or maybe somehow, because I'm empathetic, it means I'm weak. I totally rebel against that. I refuse to believe that you cannot be both compassionate and strong."*

Chapter 5:

Inner Work and Soul Health

Leadership Rule #105 - "Being Whole in Your Soul is > Being Mentally Advanced..."

Pete Scazzero, in his book "The Emotionally Healthy Leader," said that "The most important thing a leader brings to their work is themselves." As leaders, we often focus on developing our external credentials, advanced degrees, impressive resumes, and accolades. But true leadership begins within. Being whole in our souls, not just advanced in our minds, is essential for effectively navigating the complexities of human relationships and leading others with empathy, wisdom, and compassion.

Leaders who fail to cultivate internal wholeness not only hinder their own potential but also perpetuate a leadership culture that values technical expertise over emotional intelligence, exactly what helping professionals warn against, resulting in leaders who are proficient in certain skills but ill-equipped to manage the interpersonal dynamics of leadership and lead with authenticity.

The consequences of this internal neglect are staggering. According to Gallup research, organizations with leaders who prioritize well-being and emotional health see significant performance gains (we'll explore these specific metrics in Chapter 19, when discussing team cultivation). Yet despite these clear benefits, a 2023 study by the American Psychological Association found that while 81% of employees say they'll be looking for workplaces that support mental health in the future, only 43% feel their current organization prioritizes it, revealing a massive gap between what leaders say matters and what they model.

When leaders operate from a place of internal fragmentation, carrying unresolved pain, unexamined motivations, or unacknowledged limitations, they inevitably project that brokenness onto their teams. They become reactive rather than responsive, defensive rather than open, controlling rather than empowering. Their technical competence cannot compensate for their emotional deficiency.

Think of leadership like piloting a submarine. You can have the most sophisticated navigation systems, the most advanced sonar technology, and the most detailed maps of the ocean floor. Still, if a slow leak in the hull goes unaddressed, the vessel will eventually sink. The leak doesn't announce itself with alarms and flashing lights; it starts small, almost imperceptible, quietly flooding compartments while the crew focuses on their duties above. By the time the problem becomes obvious, the damage is often catastrophic. Internal wholeness works the same way.

Leaders can accumulate credentials, master processes, and deliver results for years while unresolved wounds, unchecked ambition, or unaddressed trauma quietly compromise their integrity.

The leak doesn't show up in quarterly reviews or performance metrics. It is reflected in patterns, like how they treat people when stressed, the decisions they make when threatened, and the culture they create when no one's watching.

And just like a submarine captain who ignores the leak, leaders who refuse to do the internal work will eventually find themselves, and their teams, submerged in dysfunction they could have prevented.

Scazzero also warns that "the darker side of leadership is that it can be a powerful catalyst for revealing the deepest, most hidden parts of our hearts." You can caffeinate your way through emotional fragmentation for a season, but eventually, your soul will demand attention, voluntarily through inner work, or forcibly through crisis.

Leadership Rule #44 - "Your mind is brilliant! But how is your heart?"

This question gets to the core of effective leadership. Having a high IQ can certainly provide a foundation for success, but emotional intelligence (EQ) is what truly sets effective leaders apart.

Consider a surgeon leading an operating room team. Technical expertise ensures the surgery is performed correctly. Still, emotional intelligence determines how the surgeon communicates under pressure, reassures anxious patients before the procedure, and motivates the team during long hours. A surgeon who listens empathetically to a nurse's concern or calmly redirects the team when complications arise builds trust and confidence. That emotional regulation and connection not only improve morale but also reduce errors and enhance patient outcomes.

A brilliant brain can help you master policy, process, and procedures, but it's the heart that allows you to understand and connect with people. Are you "people smart?" Someone who strives to grow in this area is constantly developing emotional intelligence, skills like empathy, self-awareness, and adaptability, so that what they know can inspire, motivate, and empower others. In the workplace, this is what turns knowledge into results and transforms a good professional into an effective leader.

Someone's heart posture, at its essence, is the internal orientation from which they engage with others. It is the foundation beneath our actions, words, and decisions. In leadership, heart posture determines whether we approach team members with curiosity or judgment, whether we listen to understand or to simply respond, and whether we see people as resources to be managed or as human beings to be valued. Two leaders can say the exact same words in a meeting, but the one with a posture of genuine care will be heard differently than the one whose heart is guarded, transactional, or self-protective. People intuitively sense the difference. They know when you're present with them versus performing for them.

This matters profoundly in workplace relationships because heart posture shapes trust in ways competence alone never can. A leader with exceptional strategic vision, but a defensive heart posture, will struggle to retain talent, inspire loyalty, or navigate conflict productively. When challenges arise, and they always do, teams look to their leader's heart, not just their mind. Do you respond with empathy when someone admits a mistake, or do you shame them? Do you genuinely celebrate a team member's success, or is envy woven into your congratulations? Do you create space for dissenting opinions, or does your ego demand agreement? These moments reveal whether your heart posture is one of scarcity (protecting your position, hoarding credit, fearing vulnerability) or abundance (lifting others, sharing authority, embracing honesty). Heart posture is what allows your brilliance to become a gift to others rather than a barrier between you and them.

The question "how is your heart" is not soft or secondary; it's diagnostic.

It asks, "Are you leading from a place of wholeness or woundedness? Security or insecurity? Service or self-interest?"

Because whatever posture your heart assumes internally will eventually express itself externally in every interaction, decision, and relationship you steward as a leader. You can polish your communication skills, attend every training, and master every framework, but if your heart posture remains closed, self-focused, or fearful, your leadership will plateau.

Conversely, a leader who tends to their heart, who does the difficult work of addressing their own pain, confronting their biases, and staying emotionally available, becomes someone people want to follow, not because they have to, but because they feel genuinely seen, valued, and believed in.

But what is the EQ of your heart?

How high is your emotional intelligence quotient when it comes to essential qualities like:

- **Integrity:** Do you operate with transparency, honesty, and ethics?

- **Self-control:** Can you manage your emotions, impulses, and reactions?

- **Compassion**: Do you genuinely care for and empathize with others?

- **Patience**: Can you tolerate frustration, delay, or difficulty with calmness and composure?

- **Humility**: Do you recognize your limitations, acknowledge your mistakes, and learn from them?

- **Accountability**: Do you take ownership of your actions, decisions, and outcomes?

As a leader, it's essential to recognize that your heart EQ is just as important as your brain IQ.

Chapter 6:

Ego and Humility

Leadership Rule #39 - "My ego will affect how we go…"

When our ego feels threatened, the brain reacts as if we're facing physical danger. The amygdala (a small part of your brain's limbic system) quickly detects the threat. At the same time, midbrain defense circuits prepare fight-or-flight responses, often overriding rational control from the prefrontal cortex. This can lead to defensive behaviors such as denial, rationalization, withdrawal, or even aggression. Because social threats like criticism or rejection activate the same neural pathways as fear, they hijack attention and impair clear thinking. Over time, chronic defensiveness can damage relationships, block learning, and increase stress. Managing ego threat requires strengthening self-awareness and emotional regulation, so the brain doesn't default to survival mode. In essence, ego threat is the mind's way of protecting identity, but unchecked, it can limit growth and connection.

One of the most destructive manifestations of ego threat is passive-aggressive behavior, an indirect form of resistance masked by superficial compliance. When leaders can't admit they're wrong or express disagreement directly, they agree publicly but sabotage privately. This pattern, which we'll address more fully in Chapter 22, reveals a fragile ego that lacks the courage to engage in conflict honestly.

Being "right" means nothing if we express it the wrong way. When we let our ego dictate our actions, we become blind to our own flaws and unwilling to admit when we're wrong. This not only hinders our ability to lead effectively but also creates a toxic environment where team members feel undervalued and untrusted.

A leader with a big ego is often driven by insecurity and a need for validation, rather than a genuine desire to serve and empower others. When we prioritize our own identity and reputation over our team's needs, we create a culture of fear and mistrust. By letting go of our ego and embracing humility, we can create a safe and supportive environment where our team can thrive.

The questions remain: Can you tell when your ego is interfering with your ability to lead and execute? How do you keep things like pride, selfish ambition, and a lack of humility in check?

Gallup reports that one in two employees has left a job to escape a manager, which strongly supports the idea that leadership behavior is a major obstacle or enabler of workplace success. Leaders with high levels of narcissism are more likely to engage in destructive behaviors, such as exploiting employees and prioritizing their own interests over the organization's.

When ego dominates, the need to be right supersedes the pursuit of truth; the desire to win eclipses the goal of mutual understanding. This dynamic opens the door for division because the ego interprets any challenge to one's position as a threat to one's identity, triggering defensive mechanisms that escalate rather than de-escalate tension. Pride, in this framework, becomes the architect of relational fracture, turning what could be productive discourse into destructive combat. Leaders operating from an ego approach to conflict ask, "How do I win?" rather than "How do we resolve this?"

In contrast, the willingness to resolve conflict authentically flows from a heart posture rooted in other-centeredness, a deliberate orientation toward the well-being and perspective of those beyond oneself. This selfless approach requires leaders to practice humility, recognizing that their viewpoint is partial, their knowledge incomplete, and their biases real. Where ego demands vindication, humility seeks understanding. Where pride insists on winning, selflessness prioritizes reconciliation and collective flourishing. Leaders who cultivate humility as a conflict-prevention tool effectively disarm the ego's tendency to turn disagreements into wars of attrition. By "checking the ego at the door," leaders signal that the purpose of these conversations transcends personal validation; it aims toward truth, growth, and unity.

This commitment transforms conflict from a destructive force into a constructive opportunity, where diverse perspectives can be honored without threatening individual worth, and where resolution becomes possible because all parties feel genuinely seen, heard, and valued. Selfishness isolates and divides; selflessness connects and heals.

Dr. Venugopal Reddy walked into the hospital boardroom with a knot in his stomach. For weeks, tension had been simmering between the doctors and the administrative staff. Meetings had turned into battlegrounds, with raised voices and defensive postures. He knew, deep down, that he wasn't helping. Every time someone challenged his decisions, his instinct was to push back, to prove he was right. The more he defended himself, the more the team fractured.

One evening, after yet another heated exchange, Dr. Reddy sat alone in his office replaying the conflict. He realized the common thread wasn't just the staff's disagreements; it was his own ego. His need to protect his authority had blinded him to the bigger picture: patient care. That night, he made a quiet promise to himself: I will lead differently.

The next morning, instead of opening the meeting with directives, he began with humility. "I realize I've been defensive," he admitted. "I want us to work together, not against each other." The room fell silent. For the first time, the staff saw vulnerability in their leader. Slowly, conversations shifted. He encouraged role clarification to ensure no one felt undermined, and he introduced emotional intelligence workshops to help the team recognize their own ego triggers.

Over time, the atmosphere transformed. Doctors and administrators began listening instead of arguing. Conflicts were addressed openly, without blame. Staff morale rose, and patients noticed the difference in care. By confronting his own ego, Dr. Reddy had unlocked a new kind of leadership, one rooted in humility, collaboration, and trust.

Leadership Rule #102 - "Be the first to be second, instead of being the second to be first…"

An effective leader should place a high importance on humility and servant leadership. "Be the first to be second" means prioritizing others' needs and interests above your own desire for recognition, power, or prestige. It's about being willing to take a supportive role, rather than always striving to be in the lead.

In his book, "The Servant Leader," James Autry writes, "Leadership is not about controlling people; it's about caring for people and being a useful resource for people." Autry's words reinforce the idea that effective leadership is rooted in humility and service, not ego or dominance. His framing of leadership as "caring for people" aligns perfectly with the concept of "be the first to be second," placing others' needs ahead of personal recognition or prestige.

By putting others first, you create opportunities for them to grow, learn, and succeed. This promotes a collaborative environment where everyone works together towards a common goal. This mindset shows that you value humility and are willing to put others' needs before your own.

On the other hand, "being the second to be first" implies a competitive, individualistic approach in which one's primary goal is to surpass others and attain the top spot. In a relay race, imagine one runner who's so focused on being the fastest that they sprint ahead without properly passing the baton. They might cross their leg of the track first, but if the baton is dropped, the whole team loses.

Here are three keys to applying Rule 102:

1.   Prioritize listening to others, rather than always trying to dominate the conversation.

2.   Be willing to support and amplify others' ideas, even if they're not your own.

3.   Embody servant leadership by putting the needs of your team, organization, or community ahead of your own interests.

Nelson Mandela once said, *"It is better to lead from behind and to put others in front, especially when you celebrate victory when nice things occur. You take the front line when danger arises. Then people will appreciate your leadership."*

Chapter 7:

Purpose and Identity

Frank Viola once wrote, "Purpose is the father of commitment. It is the mother of motivation. It is the parent of passion. Purpose provides meaning. It instills direction, inspiration, and unity. It also brings fulfillment. Without a discovery of purpose, everyday life becomes oppressive and demeaning. We can find little in it except the next thing, which is virtually indistinguishable from the last thing. Purpose rescues us from this mundane existence."

These words capture what many leaders experience but struggle to articulate: the suffocating emptiness of achievement without meaning. You can climb every rung of the corporate ladder, accumulate every credential, and deliver every quarterly result, yet still feel the gnawing sense that you're living someone else's definition of success. This isn't a failure of ambition or work ethic. It's the inevitable consequence of confusing profession with purpose.

Leadership Rule #29 - "Your purpose can be exercised in your profession, but your profession will never be your purpose…"

It's Friday! As you prepare to finish your workweek strong, remember that the importance of our role is not so much in "what we do" as in "why" we do it. Occupation is an external expression, whereas purpose resides within, an intrinsic north star guiding one's existence. So, don't just finish the work week, but continue to fulfill the purpose for which you are at work.

For many of us, it's easy to measure success by tasks completed or deadlines met. Yet true fulfillment comes from aligning those tasks with a deeper sense of purpose. When leaders and professionals keep their "why" at the forefront, even routine responsibilities become opportunities to live out values, inspire others, and contribute to something larger than themselves.

Purpose transforms work from a checklist into a calling, reminding us that our profession is simply the platform through which we express our deeper mission. By recognizing that purpose transcends job titles, we avoid the trap of defining ourselves solely by what we do. Instead, we cultivate resilience, motivation, and impact that extend beyond the workweek, ensuring that our efforts remain meaningful and sustainable.

This distinction becomes even more critical when we consider the brevity of life itself. We spend decades building careers, climbing ladders, and accumulating accomplishments, but at the end of our days, what we did for a living rarely defines our legacy. What endures is how we made people feel, the lives we touched, the values we embodied, and the purpose we carried out through our work. A manager who sees their role merely as overseeing tasks will be forgotten. But a leader who sees their role as cultivating people, creating belonging, and serving something beyond themselves leaves an imprint that outlasts their tenure.

The question is not whether you showed up to work; it's whether you showed up on purpose. Did you bring your full humanity to the role? Did you allow your deeper calling to shape how you led, communicated, and connected? Or did you simply perform the mechanics of your job while your soul remained disengaged?

Understanding that "why" we are here matters more than "what" we do can liberate us from the tyranny of productivity and performance. It reframes our paradigm from leadership as stewardship, not of budgets, timelines, or deliverables, but of human dignity, potential, and flourishing. Your title is temporary, but your influence is eternal.

For C-suite readers who only measure success purely by financial metrics, consider this: Purpose-driven companies outperform their competitors by 42% in revenue growth, and employees who find meaning in their work deliver 50% higher productivity.

The bottom line you're chasing is directly tied to the purpose your people are living out or lacking. Investing in purpose isn't soft leadership; it's the smartest business decision you can make.

Sheryl Sandberg articulated this when she said that "Leadership is about making others better as a result of your presence and making sure that impact lasts in your absence."

Leadership Rule #33 - "Everybody is called to be a leader, but not everyone learns how to lead…"

This underscores the universal potential for influence and impact inherent within everyone. However, actualizing this potential requires cultivating self-awareness, empathy, and wisdom, distinguishing leaders who inspire and uplift from those who merely hold power. Ultimately, leadership is not about titles or authority but about harnessing one's unique gifts to serve and elevate others.

It takes courage to lead others. But courage doesn't mean fearlessness; it means a willingness to persevere in the face of fear. Let the lesson begin with you and your journey to overcome your own fears, prejudices, and preconceived notions.

Everyone who gets a license is technically "called" to be a driver, but not everyone becomes a good driver. Some people know about mechanics, how to start the engine, shift gears, and follow GPS directions. Still, they haven't developed essential skills such as anticipating traffic, staying calm under pressure, or being considerate of others on the road.

Leadership works the same way. The title or opportunity may be given, but true effectiveness comes from learning how to navigate challenges, care for people, and guide them safely toward a destination.

This journey requires unlearning. Much of what we've been taught, consciously or unconsciously, about how to view, categorize, and deal with people must be examined and often discarded. We inherit belief systems from family, culture, early managers, and societal norms that shape how we perceive others' competence, worthiness, trustworthiness, and potential. Some of these inherited beliefs serve us well; many do not. The leader who was taught that showing emotion is a sign of weakness must unlearn this to practice empathy. The leader raised in environments where hierarchy equates with dominance must unlearn this to embrace servant leadership. The leader who absorbed the message that certain types of people are "less than" must unlearn it to lead toward equality and inclusion.

Unlearning is not erasing your past; it's examining what you've internalized, testing it against truth and effectiveness, and choosing to release what no longer serves you or the people you lead. This process is uncomfortable because it challenges identity, raises questions about long-held assumptions, and requires admitting that some of what we believed was wrong. But without peeling back the layers of what we were once taught, we cannot teach others differently. We simply replicate the same flawed patterns, biases, and limiting beliefs that were passed down to us. The greatest leaders recognize that becoming a better leader often means becoming a better student, willing to sit in the discomfort of unlearning to create space for new, healthier, more effective ways of seeing and serving people.

Chapter 8:

Stewardship and Responsibility

Leadership Rule #101 - You're not the owner, you're the caretaker..."

Stewardship refers to the responsible management and care of resources, assets, or talents entrusted to one's care. A steward manages and oversees assets that belong to others, aiming to preserve, protect, and increase their value.

The word "steward" comes from the Old English words "stig" (house) and "weard" (guardian). In medieval times, a steward was a high-ranking servant responsible for managing a noble's household, estate, and finances.

In leadership, stewardship is essential because it recognizes that leaders are not owners, but rather caretakers of the organization, its resources, and its people. Good stewards prioritize the well-being and success of the organization and its stakeholders over personal interests.

Effective stewardship in leadership involves:

- Accountability
- Responsibility

- Transparency
- Humility

And here's the fruit from one who stewards their leadership role well: Stakeholders develop trust in the leader and the organization. Employees become more engaged and motivated when they know their leader cares about their well-being. The organization becomes more sustainable as the leader prioritizes long-term success over short-term gains. The leader leaves a lasting, positive legacy by stewarding a strong foundation for future success.

A general contractor doesn't own their crews. They steward them. The laborers, carpenters, electricians, and plumbers on your site aren't your property; they're people entrusted to your leadership, often by subcontractors who expect you to create an environment where their workers can succeed and stay safe. True stewardship in construction leadership means recognizing that every person on your jobsite has been placed under your temporary care, and that how you treat them shapes not just this project but their entire career trajectory and livelihood.

When a GC notices a young laborer struggling with the physical demands of the job and connects them with an experienced mentor rather than just firing them, that's the stewardship of people. When a superintendent recognizes that a skilled tradesperson is underutilized and advocates for them to assume greater responsibility, that's stewardship. When a project manager shields their foremen from unnecessary owner drama so they can focus on leading their crews well, that's stewardship. When a leader ensures every worker, regardless of which subcontractor badge they wear, leaves the site safely to return to their families, that's stewardship.

With skilled labor shortages forcing the industry to compete for every qualified worker, the temptation is to view people as interchangeable resources or treat them as disposable when they don't perform immediately. But effective leaders understand that they are stewards and caretakers of people's careers, confidence, and professional development. When you steward people well, they don't just complete your project; they grow under your leadership, speak highly of working with you, and return for the next job. Poor stewardship burns through people. Good stewardship builds loyalty, develops talent, and creates a reputation that attracts the best crews even in tight labor markets.

Leadership Rule #16 - "Respect rights, appreciate privileges…"

In the workplace, a right is an inherent entitlement, such as the right to fair treatment and safety. In contrast, a privilege is a benefit granted by the employer, such as flexible hours or remote work. Recognizing that having a job itself is a privilege, not a right, underscores the importance of gratitude and humility in leadership. Leaders who understand this distinction foster a culture of appreciation and responsibility, inspiring their teams to value their roles and contribute meaningfully. This perspective encourages a balanced approach to leadership, where privileges are earned and rights are respected.

If people fail to understand the distinction between rights and privileges in the workplace, the impact can be significant. Employees may come to view every benefit as an entitlement, fostering resentment when those benefits are adjusted or removed. This mindset erodes gratitude and can lead to disengagement, entitlement-driven conflict, and a lack of accountability. Leaders who don't clarify this difference risk cultivating a culture where appreciation is scarce and responsibility is diminished, ultimately weakening morale and productivity.

On the other hand, when leaders emphasize that rights must always be protected while privileges are earned and appreciated, they create a healthier balance. Without this understanding, organizations may struggle with high turnover, reduced trust, and a workforce that undervalues the opportunities offered. Recognizing employment itself as a privilege encourages humility, resilience, and a stronger sense of purpose, while misunderstanding it can lead to entitlement, dissatisfaction, and stagnation.

Sarah was a team leader in Manchester, UK, whose department faced significant restructuring during a particularly difficult economic period. She had been with the company for twelve years and had worked her way up from an entry-level position to managing a team of fifteen. When budget cuts forced the organization to eliminate several long-standing perks, including annual bonuses that employees had come to expect and subsidized gym memberships that had been in place for a decade, the reaction was swift and intense. Several team members began circulating complaints via internal messaging platforms. Some threatened to leave, while others openly expressed bitterness during meetings.

Sarah called a team meeting where she did something unexpected: she acknowledged their frustration honestly, validated that the changes were challenging, and then shared her own story. She spoke about growing up on a council estate in Liverpool, watching her father lose his job during the early 1990s recession, and struggling for 2 years to find work. She reminded her team that while the perks they'd lost were valuable and had been genuinely appreciated, they still had what her father had desperately wanted: stable employment, fair wages, and the dignity of meaningful work. She made it clear that their rights, safe working conditions, fair treatment, and respect would never be negotiated away, and that she would fight for those as fiercely as ever. But she also asked them to consider whether they had confused privileges with entitlements, and whether that confusion was blinding them to the opportunity they still possessed.

The shift wasn't immediate, but over the following weeks, the tone changed. Team members began expressing gratitude for what remained rather than fixating on what was lost. Productivity stabilized, and several employees who had threatened to leave instead doubled down on their contributions, recognizing that their roles were not guaranteed commodities but opportunities to be stewarded well. Sarah's willingness to lead with vulnerability and clarity helped her team recalibrate their perspective, transforming what could have been a morale crisis into a moment of collective maturity and renewed purpose.

This is the essence of effective leadership: The ability to guide people through difficulty with empathy and clarity, protecting their rights while helping them distinguish between entitlement and appreciation.

Sarah demonstrated all three pillars that define The Helpful Leader: emotional intelligence, as she recognized her team's frustration and responded with vulnerability rather than defensiveness. Effective communication, in articulating the distinction between rights and privileges without diminishing either, and conflict resolution, in transforming potential resentment into renewed purpose.

Leaders who master this balance don't just manage change; they steward people through it, cultivating resilience, gratitude, and a deeper understanding of what it means to show up with humility in the workplace. This is how privileges are honored, rights are protected, and teams emerge stronger rather than embittered.

Chapter 9:

Knowing Your People

Leadership Rule #7 - "KYP aids in your KPI's…"

In the book "Winning Well" by Karin Hurt and David Dye, the authors say, "You can't lead people you don't know." KYP (Knowing Your Personnel) is a catalyst for social connection and emotional intelligence in effective leadership. Research in behavioral science has consistently shown that leaders who prioritize building relationships with their team members are more successful in motivating and inspiring them.

But knowing your people isn't just about remembering names or understanding job roles. It's about understanding what drives human beings at a fundamental level. Psychologist Abraham Maslow provided one of the most enduring frameworks for this in his hierarchy of needs (see next page). Maslow proposed that humans are motivated by five levels of needs, arranged hierarchically:

The Helpful Leader   James Oyola

Self-Actualization Needs
Self-fulfillment, actualizing
one's potential

Self-Esteem Needs
High self-respect, self-approval, esteem
of others, achievement, competency,
reputation, prestige, status

Belonging and Love Needs
Friendship, affection, acceptance and
identification with others

Safety Needs
Structure, order, law, security, stability,
protection, freedom from fear, anxiety, chaos

Physiological Needs
food, water, air

Maslow's Hierarchy of Needs

At the base are **physiological needs** (food, water, air). Without these, nothing else matters. Once met, people seek **safety** (security, stability, protection from harm). With safety established, they pursue **belonging and love** (friendship, affection, acceptance within the community). Meeting these needs fosters a drive for **self-esteem** (achievement, recognition, respect, status). Only when these four levels are met can people pursue self-actualization, realize their full potential, and become the best version of themselves.

Why does this matter for leaders? You cannot expect someone to perform at a higher level in the hierarchy if their foundational needs are unmet.

If an employee feels unsafe (fearing humiliation, arbitrary firing, or scapegoating), they cannot focus on achievement or innovation. If they don't feel like they belong (excluded, unseen, marginalized), they won't invest emotional energy in the team's success. If their basic need for respect isn't met, they won't care about self-actualization or organizational goals. They're too busy trying to secure the lower-level needs you've left unaddressed.

This is where Knowing Your People becomes strategic, not just relational. When you genuinely know someone, their stressors, their strengths, their fears, their aspirations, you can identify which level of the hierarchy they're operating from and what needs require attention. A team member who's distracted isn't necessarily lazy; they might be operating from safety needs (worried about job security) or belonging needs (feeling isolated from the team). A high performer who's suddenly disengaged isn't necessarily burned out; they may have reached a self-esteem plateau and need recognition or new challenges to feel valued.

Effective leaders use Maslow's framework diagnostically, asking, "Where is this person on the hierarchy right now? What need is unmet that's preventing them from contributing fully?"

Once you can answer those questions, you can address the underlying barrier rather than merely demanding improved performance.

A Harvard Business Review study found that leaders perceived as empathetic and understanding were more likely to have high-performing teams. By investing time and effort in getting to know their team members, leaders can develop a deeper understanding of their needs, preferences, and motivations, ultimately leading to more effective leadership and better outcomes.

Knowing Your Personnel (KYP) extends far beyond remembering names or understanding job roles; it requires leaders to develop the emotional and observational acuity necessary to detect early warning signs of conflict before they escalate. Research indicates that as much as 65% of interpersonal communication is conveyed nonverbally; therefore, effective leaders must become fluent in reading body language, facial expressions, tone shifts, and behavioral cues.

These nonverbal cues often reveal what words cannot, such as a team member suddenly crossing their arms during meetings, an employee whose eye contact has diminished, or a colleague whose tone has become clipped and distant.

These subtle shifts are not random; they are signaling that tension, disengagement, or interpersonal conflict may be simmering beneath the surface.

Leaders may not always be able to control events, but they should be able to control the behavior they exhibit in response. According to communication scholar Albert Mehrabian, approximately 7% of our emotional understanding of others is attributed to their words, while 38% and 55%, respectively, are attributed to their verbal tone and facial expression. We cannot overestimate the power of nonverbal cues.

When leaders cultivate relational awareness, they position themselves to intervene proactively rather than reactively. This proactive approach is critical because the goal of conflict detection is not to single out or punish one individual, but to protect the environment and everyone within it. A leader who notices tension between two team members, for example, should address the issue not as a matter of assigning blame, but as a means of preserving psychological safety and team cohesion. Research reveals that 45% of employees reported being frequently or occasionally confused by inconsistent cues from their supervisors, and more than 94% reported feeling frustrated or distrustful when confronted with inconsistent communications.

This data underscores the reality that unresolved tension, whether interpersonal or stemming from mixed messages, erodes trust across the entire team, not just between the directly involved parties. When leaders ignore early signs of conflict, they inadvertently allow a toxic dynamic to spread, impacting morale, productivity, and collaboration across the organization.

Cultural intelligence is key to truly knowing your people (KYP). What motivates employees varies across cultural contexts, so your approach must adapt accordingly. In individualist cultures, the focus is on personal goals and individual recognition, while respecting boundaries. In collectivist cultures, the emphasis is on family, team dynamics, and framing success as serving the group. High-context cultures require reading between the lines and building trust gradually, whereas low-context cultures value direct communication and clarity.

Power distance also matters in high power distance cultures; employees may hesitate to speak up, so private conversations and intentional trust-building are essential. In low-power-distance cultures, expect direct feedback and informality as signs of engagement. The universal principle remains the same: understand what motivates your people and tailor your questions and methods to their cultural norms. Cultural intelligence isn't optional; it's the foundation for effective leadership.

Imagine a gardener tending to a variety of plants. Each plant has different needs—some require more sunlight, others thrive in shade. Some need frequent watering, while others prefer dry soil. If the gardener doesn't take the time to know each plant, they might water them all the same or place them all in the sun, and many would wither. But by learning the unique requirements of each plant, the gardener helps them flourish together, creating a thriving garden.

One of the most damaging phrases in corporate leadership is also one of the most common: "Leave your problems at the door."

On the surface, it sounds reasonable, even professional. The implication is that work requires focus, and personal issues can distract from productivity.

What this phrase communicates is far more destructive: "Your humanity is inconvenient to me. Pretend you're fine so I don't have to deal with you as a person."

Leaders who default to this language are operating from a fundamental misunderstanding of how human beings function. And I am almost positive about the leaders who say this, that they don't follow the principle, in that way, all the time. We are not machines that can compartmentalize pain, anxiety, grief, or stress simply because we've crossed a threshold into a workspace.

Neuroscience confirms what most of us intuitively know. That our brains don't have an "off switch" for emotions.

When someone is dealing with a sick parent, a financial crisis, a relationship breakdown, or a mental health struggle, that reality doesn't vanish because they clocked in. It follows them into meetings, into their decision-making, into their interactions with colleagues. Pretending otherwise doesn't make it disappear; it just forces people to pretend to be normal while drowning internally.

The "leave your problems at the door" leader is telling their team, "I don't want to know what you're going through. I don't have the capacity, interest, or emotional bandwidth to acknowledge your struggle. Just show up, do your job, and keep the suffering to yourself."

This approach may appear efficient in the short term, but it erodes trust, breeds resentment, and ultimately damages productivity far more than the honesty it seeks to suppress. Employees who feel compelled to conceal their struggles become disengaged. They stop bringing their full selves to work because they've learned that only a sanitized, emotionally sterile version of themselves is acceptable. Over time, this creates a culture where people show up physically but check out mentally and emotionally, precisely the opposite of what the leader intended.

Contrast this with the leader who says, "I know you're carrying something heavy right now. Let's talk about

how we can help you manage it while you're here, so it doesn't consume you during work hours, but also so you don't feel like you must pretend it doesn't exist."

This leader isn't suggesting people ignore their problems. They're offering a framework to try to put in your mental locker while you're at work. The distinction is critical. A mental locker isn't denial; it's a temporary, intentional compartmentalization that acknowledges the struggle while creating space to focus on tasks that require attention.

It says, "Your problem is real. It matters. And part of how we support you is by helping you create boundaries that protect your wellbeing."

This approach requires more from the leader. It requires emotional intelligence, empathy, and the willingness to engage in uncomfortable conversations. It means asking, "What's going on?" and listening to the answer.

It means checking in periodically, asking, "How are you managing today? Do you need to step away for a few minutes?"

It means understanding that some days, people will only have 70% to give, and that's okay, because they're still showing up and trying. The mental locker approach doesn't lower standards or eliminate accountability; it recognizes that humans perform best when they feel seen, supported, and given tools to manage their reality, rather than being forced to deny it.

Here's what this looks like in practice:

Monica, a team lead in your department, comes to you visibly distressed one morning. You know from previous conversations that her father has been battling cancer. A "leave your problems at the door" leader might say, "I'm sorry to hear that, but we have a big presentation today. I need you to be focused." That response shuts down vulnerability, communicates that her pain is merely an inconvenience, and leaves Monica to push through the day while internally collapsing. She'll likely resent you for it, and her performance, despite her best efforts, will suffer because she's expending enormous energy just trying to hold it together.

A helpful leader responds differently. "I can see you're struggling today. What's happening with your dad?" **After listening, they continue.** "Here's what I'm thinking. We do need you in the presentation, and I know you're capable of doing it well. But let's be realistic about what you need today. Can you put this in your mental locker for the next two hours while we present the information to the group? After that, take the rest of the afternoon off. Go be with your family. We'll cover things here." This leader has acknowledged the struggle, maintained the work requirement, and created space for Monica to manage both. She knows her pain isn't being dismissed. She has been given permission to focus temporarily and has been offered support.

The result? Monica attends the presentation, delivers well because she feels supported rather than alone, and leaves with gratitude and loyalty toward a leader who saw her as a person rather than just an employee.

This isn't about coddling people or lowering expectations. It's about recognizing that the teams that perform best are those that feel safe bringing their whole selves to work, including their struggles. When you create a culture where people can say, "I'm not okay today, but I'm here, and I'll do my best," you build resilience. When you offer tools like the mental locker, a framework for temporary compartmentalization paired with genuine support, you give people autonomy over their own emotional management while signaling that you're in their corner.

The "leave your problems at the door" leader might get compliance, but they'll never earn loyalty. They'll never inspire the kind of effort that comes from people who genuinely want to show up for a leader who has shown up for them. When turnover statistics indicate that a lack of managerial support is among the top reasons employees leave, this distinction becomes more than philosophical; it's strategic. The leader who helps people navigate their struggles while keeping them accountable to their commitments builds teams that endure. The leader who demands that people pretend they're fine builds teams that fragment under pressure.

As we explored earlier in this chapter, knowing your people means understanding what's beneath the surface, the 90% of the iceberg you can't see. You can't access that depth if you've signaled that you don't want to know what people are carrying. The mental locker approach opens the door to honest conversation.

It says, "I see you. I know life is hard sometimes. Let's figure out how to navigate this together."

That's not a weakness, it's wisdom. That's not lowering the bar; it's recognizing that human beings perform best when they feel supported, not abandoned. Leaders who understand this distinction build teams that endure.

You can't nurture growth if you don't understand the individuals you're leading. Just as the gardener's success depends on knowing their plants, a leader's success depends on knowing their people, their strengths, struggles, and motivations. That knowledge enables leaders to inspire, support, and cultivate high performance.

However, knowing your personnel is only half the equation; effective leaders must also know themselves and be acutely aware of their nonverbal communication. While you're reading your team's body language, they're reading yours. And often, leaders are completely unconscious of the messages they send.

Consider these common scenarios:

A team member proposes an idea in a meeting. Before you even respond verbally, your face scrunches slightly, which is what you experience internally as your 'thinking face' while processing the suggestion. However, to the person speaking, that expression reads as disapproval or skepticism, immediately undermining their willingness to contribute in the next meeting. Or perhaps someone presents factually incorrect information, and you let out a small chuckle or smirk, not because you're trying to mock them, but because you're surprised or caught off guard. Yet that unconscious reaction humiliates the person and signals to everyone watching that mistakes will be met with ridicule rather than correction.

Leaders must audit their nonverbal habits.

Do you cross your arms when listening (which can be read as closed-off or defensive)? Do you check your phone when someone's talking (signaling that their words do not matter)? Do you sigh heavily when interrupted (communicating frustration and impatience)? Do you maintain eye contact consistently, or do your eyes glaze over when certain people speak? These micro-behaviors, completely unintentional, carry enormous weight because your position amplifies their impact.

We'll explore this 'below the surface' dynamic more fully in Chapter 21 with the Iceberg Model of Leadership.

Leadership Rule #158 - "Show Them That You Care..."

U.S. President Theodore Roosevelt said, "People don't care how much you know until they know how much you care." Empathy is crucial for effective leadership, enabling leaders to build strong relationships, communicate effectively, and make informed decisions. To achieve results in a team dynamic, the leader needs to know the team and the strengths/weaknesses of all team members.

In his book, "Emotional Intelligence: Why IT Can Matter More Than IQ," author Daniel Goleman writes, "The ability to control impulses is the base of will and character. By the same token, the root of altruism lies in empathy, the ability to read emotions in others; lacking a sense of another's need or despair, there is no caring. And if there are any two moral stances that our times call for, they are precisely these, self-restraint and compassion."

Narcissism and self-centeredness often pose the biggest threats to empathy. When we're too focused on our own needs, feelings, and perspectives, it can be harder to truly listen, understand, and connect with others.

Other factors include:

• **Technology overload:** Constantly being plugged in can desensitize us to others' emotions.

• **Stress and burnout**: When we're overwhelmed, it's tough to prioritize others' feelings.

- **Biases and assumptions**: Preconceived notions can lead to misunderstandings and a lack of empathy.

If leaders fail to demonstrate empathy and genuine care for their teams, the consequences can be detrimental to a company's culture and performance. Without empathy, employees may feel undervalued, misunderstood, or disconnected, thereby eroding trust and weakening morale. Over time, this leads to disengagement, higher turnover, and reduced collaboration, because people are less likely to give their best when they don't feel respected or supported.

From a business standpoint, ignoring your team's strengths and weaknesses leads to poor decision-making and ineffective execution. Leaders who don't invest in relationships often miss critical insights, overlook hidden talents, and fail to anticipate challenges. This not only stifles innovation but also creates inefficiencies that directly impact productivity and profitability. In short, when leaders neglect empathy, they undermine both the human and operational foundations of the company.

"Empathy is the antidote to shame, and it's the heart of connection," - Tarana Burke.

Chapter 10:

People Over Process

Leadership Rule #6 - "It's cool if you know processes, but do you know people?"

This ties directly to the principle of "know your people (KYP)" we went over in Chapter 9. Processes may create structure, but without a true understanding of the individuals who operate within those processes, leaders miss the opportunity to unlock the human potential that drives results. KYP means going beyond surface-level interactions to intentionally learn about each person's strengths, weaknesses, and motivations. When leaders invest in this relational knowledge, they can align tasks with talents, provide support where it's needed, and empower team members to contribute in ways that maximize both individual growth and collective success.

Effective leaders recognize that processes are merely tools, but people are the driving force behind success. Knowing your team members' strengths, weaknesses, and motivations is crucial to unlocking their full potential. This can occur only through intentional relationship-building, keen observation, and the goal of positioning everyone for the best opportunity to contribute effectively to the team's overall success. While processes provide a necessary framework, it's the human element that brings creativity, innovation, and resilience to the table, and that's what truly sets exceptional leaders apart. We'll explore how to apply this understanding to individual strengths and team composition in Chapters 15 and 16.

Consider the difference between reading sheet music and playing an instrument. A musician can memorize every note, understand tempo markings, and follow dynamic instructions perfectly, but that technical knowledge alone doesn't create music that moves people. What transforms notation into artistry is the musician's intuitive feel for phrasing, their ability to interpret emotional nuance, and their sensitivity to how each performance should breathe differently, depending on the audience and the room's acoustics. Two pianists can play the exact same Chopin nocturne with flawless technique, but one performance will leave you unmoved while the other brings you to tears. The difference lies not in their knowledge of the process. It lies in their understanding of the human experience they seek to convey.

Leadership operates on the same principle. You can master every operational workflow, memorize every policy manual, and execute every procedure with precision. Still, if you don't understand the people who interpret and execute those processes, your leadership will feel mechanical and disconnected. A process might dictate how to handle customer complaints, but only by knowing your team can you discern that Maria thrives under pressure and should handle the most difficult escalations. At the same time, David needs gradual exposure to conflict because past experiences have made confrontation anxiety-inducing for him. The process is the same; the application must be personalized. Leaders who ignore this reality treat their teams like interchangeable parts in a machine, wondering why morale suffers and turnover increases despite "doing everything by the book."

The irony is that leaders often retreat into process-oriented management precisely because knowing people feels too complex, too time-consuming, or too emotionally demanding. It's easier to enforce a standardized protocol than to invest in understanding why that protocol might not work equally well for everyone on your team. But this avoidance comes at a steep cost. When you don't know your people, you miss the warning signs that someone is burning out, overlook talent that could be developed, inadvertently trigger past wounds through careless comments, and create an environment where people feel like expendable resources rather than valued contributors.

The most effective leaders understand that the time spent genuinely getting to know their team isn't a distraction from the work; it is the work. Because once you truly know your people, everything else, delegation, motivation, conflict resolution, and performance management, becomes exponentially more effective.

Leadership Rule #31 - "Being an effective leader is less about being nice and more about being intentional…"

As a leader, I believe effectiveness is not about being a nice person but about being intentional. Intentional leadership means making deliberate, thoughtful decisions about how you invest your time, attention, and influence, rather than simply reacting to whatever demands the day brings. It's about taking the time to truly know and understand each member of our team, not just their strengths and weaknesses, but their motivations, values, and goals. Most leaders do not invest in this way because they may lack the bandwidth to do so, given their many responsibilities. Or maybe they just don't understand the benefits of this principle. But it's essential for the health of the team to understand each part in this way.

Through intentional leadership, we'll unlock our collective potential and achieve greatness together. At the same time, this positions us to identify potential red flags and to work with the person for their benefit and the team's.

This principle drives high sales efficiency and ROI because intentional leadership focuses on purposeful actions aligned with business goals, rather than merely maintaining superficial harmony. Being "nice" may create short-term comfort, but it doesn't necessarily improve performance. Intentional leaders, however, deliberately invest in knowing their people, setting clear expectations, and aligning strengths with opportunities, all of which directly impact sales outcomes.

They adopt a "behavior-based" coaching model and strive to accomplish the following:

- **Targeted coaching**: Intentional leaders identify individual skill gaps and provide tailored support, accelerating sales readiness and reducing wasted effort.

- **Strategic alignment**: By focusing on intentional goals, leaders ensure sales activities are tied to measurable business objectives, thereby increasing conversion rates and revenue impact.

- **Resource optimization**: Intentional leadership prioritizes high-value opportunities and eliminates inefficiencies, leading to better use of time, tools, and talent.

- **Employee engagement**: Teams led with purpose feel valued and motivated, which boosts productivity and lowers turnover, both critical to sustaining ROI.

This approach is the difference between a leader who schedules one-on-ones because the calendar prompts them versus a leader who uses that time to ask specific, meaningful questions designed to understand what's happening beneath the surface. Intentional leaders don't wait for problems to escalate before addressing them; they proactively observe patterns, seek out quiet voices, and create space for honest conversation before crises emerge. It's leadership that operates from a plan, not from panic, from purpose, not from pressure.

Consider Sam, an executive based in Los Angeles, California, leading a sales team in Shanghai. A "nice" leader might send friendly emails, avoid difficult conversations to maintain harmony, and assume that politeness equals good leadership. But an intentional leader recognizes that what reads as "direct feedback" in American culture can be perceived as public humiliation in Chinese business culture, where saving face is paramount. Instead of offering correction in a team meeting, which might seem efficient, Sam schedules private conversations, frames feedback as collaborative problem-solving rather than criticism, and takes time to understand each team member's family obligations during Chinese New Year, recognizing that personal life deeply affects professional commitment in collectivist cultures.

Intentional leadership here isn't about being nice; it's about being culturally intelligent, contextually aware, and purposeful in every interaction to build trust and drive results.

This kind of intentionality requires research, humility, and ongoing learning. Sam doesn't assume his leadership style will translate seamlessly across cultures. He studies how respect is communicated in China, then he asks questions about local business norms, and adjusts his approach based on what he learns. He understands that leadership effectiveness isn't measured by how comfortable he feels in his own methods, but by whether his team feels seen, valued, and empowered to succeed within their cultural context.

That's intentional leadership: Making conscious, informed choices that prioritize the growth and success of your people, even when it means stepping outside your comfort zone and leading in ways that may feel unfamiliar but are far more effective.

Chapter 11:

Respect and Recognition

Leadership Rule #11 - "An effective leader acknowledges everyone in their business from data entry to executive management..."

In my experience, I've seen situations in which senior leaders ignore frontline employees or see through them, yet prioritize someone of their rank or higher. This is unhealthy and, indirectly, reflects the value that the leader places on people. As mentioned in Chapter 9, one of the biggest needs of any human is the desire to be seen. Leadership is not about being on top of the hierarchy; it's about being willing to listen, learn, and lift others up, regardless of their title or position. When leaders fail to acknowledge and value the contributions of their frontline employees, they not only miss vital insights and ideas but also risk fostering a culture of disengagement and disillusionment.

Let's be real. We can all spot fake energy from a mile away. Gen Z and younger Millennials especially have a finely tuned detector for performative leadership, the kind where someone remembers your name only when higher-ups are watching or suddenly becomes interested in your ideas during the all-hands meeting but ghosts you in the breakroom. You know the vibe. It's the leader who'll reply to the VP's Slack message in under a minute but leaves your question on read for three days. That inconsistency doesn't just feel bad; it signals exactly where you rank in their mental org chart.

And here's the thing: That hierarchy isn't just outdated leadership; it's bad business. The people closest to the work, the ones answering customer complaints at 11 P.M., coding through bugs at 2 A.M., processing invoices that keep the lights on, those are the people who know what's breaking and what's working. Ignoring them isn't just disrespectful; it's strategically stupid.

Think about it like this: You wouldn't build a friendship where you only showed up when you needed something, right? You wouldn't follow a content creator who only engaged with verified accounts in the comments. So why would anyone stay loyal to a leader who treats them like an NPC (Non-Player Character) in their career story? This leader treats employees as if they're just background characters, existing to serve the leader's advancement. The best workplaces feel less like rigid corporate pyramids and more like collaborative crews where everyone's role matters.

When leaders make a habit of recognizing contributions across the board, not just during performance reviews or when they need a favor, they create the kind of culture people want to be part of. It's not about being everyone's best friend or throwing pizza parties to mask systemic issues. It's about consistently showing that you see the work being done, you respect the people doing it, and you're genuinely curious about them.

A great example of this is the story of Howard Schultz, the former CEO of Starbucks. During his tenure, Schultz made a point of visiting stores regularly and engaging with baristas, asking for their feedback and ideas. One such interaction led to the creation of the Pumpkin Spice Latte, which became a huge success for the company.

Schultz's willingness to listen to and value the contributions of his frontline employees not only led to innovation but also fostered a culture of inclusivity and empowerment within the organization.

Herb Kelleher, co-founder and longtime CEO of Southwest Airlines, was famous for acknowledging everyone in the company, from baggage handlers to executives. One Christmas, instead of sending gifts to his top management team, he personally wrote thousands of thank-you notes to frontline employees. He believed that the company's success depended not just on strategy but on the daily efforts of those who checked tickets, loaded luggage, and answered phones. His consistent recognition of every role created a culture of loyalty and enthusiasm that became a cornerstone of Southwest's profitability and customer satisfaction. Under Kelleher's leadership, Southwest grew into the largest domestic airline in the United States, with a reputation for affordability and customer service.

Leadership Rule #145 - "In a position of leadership, you can't not be a morning person."

I understand that some of us show up to the office with a million things on our mind, meetings (scheduled/unscheduled), personal life, work projects, etc., and our focus can remain on us within that first hour of our morning once we get to work.

A simple "good morning" is more than politeness; it signals recognition, belonging, and respect. Over time, these micro-interactions compound into stronger trust, better teamwork, and higher engagement. Since engagement is statistically linked to 21% higher profitability and 17% higher productivity (Gallup data), greetings indirectly contribute to measurable ROI.

My encouragement: The minute you walk into the office, be a morning person. What does that mean? Greet your team. Say hello. Take a few minutes to ask someone how they are doing. The opposite is walking into the office and going straight to your area. Making eye contact with your staff but not acknowledging them can unintentionally give your team the wrong understanding. We don't want to do that, especially if you manage teams outside the U.S. and engage with people from other cultures.

This aligns with what was discussed in previous chapters regarding self-awareness, self-regulation, and the need to assess what occurs in our own hearts. Inc.com also highlights social psychology research from Tufts University showing that even small gestures, such as saying "hello," build social connections, reduce stress, and increase collaboration.

Respecting everyone doesn't always mean treating everyone identically. In hierarchical cultures, respect may be demonstrated by prioritizing seniority, using appropriate titles, and adhering to protocol. This isn't discrimination; it's honoring cultural norms that create stability and clarity. The principle of "seeing everyone" remains; the expression adapts to context. Please don't make the same mistake that I made in Jamaica.

Leadership Rule #116 "Your Influence Isn't Limited by Your Org Chart…"

One of the most limiting beliefs in corporate leadership is the notion that your leadership responsibility ends at the boundary of your department. Managers often operate as if their influence and obligations extend only to those who report directly to them, or at most to those within their immediate functional area. This territorial approach to leadership creates silos, stifles collaboration, and fundamentally misunderstands what it means to lead as a servant leader.

True leadership transcends organizational charts, job titles, and departmental boundaries. It recognizes that every interaction, regardless of hierarchy or function, is an opportunity to serve, encourage, and make a lasting impact.

Consider how work actually happens in organizations. Projects don't succeed because one department operates in isolation; they succeed because cross-functional teams collaborate, share knowledge, and support one another. The marketing campaign doesn't launch without an IT infrastructure. The sales team can't close deals without product development delivering quality. Operations can't function smoothly without facilities maintenance, ensuring the environment is safe and operational. Every role is interconnected, and yet many leaders act as if the people outside their department are someone else's concern. This mindset not only limits your influence but also reveals a fundamental misunderstanding of servant leadership.

Servant leadership, at its core, is about seeing and valuing people across all aspects of the organization. Not just the people you manage. Not just the people who can advance your career. Not just the people in roles like yours. All people. The maintenance worker who empties your trash at night, or the receptionist who greets visitors every morning. The finance analyst who processes your expense reports, or the delivery driver who brings supplies to your building. These individuals are not peripheral to your leadership; they are human beings whose dignity, worth, and contributions deserve recognition, regardless of whether they appear anywhere on your org chart.

Here's the practical reality: Your reputation as a leader is shaped not just by how you treat your direct reports, but by how you treat everyone. People across the organization watch how you interact with those who have no power to benefit or harm your career. Do you acknowledge the custodian in the hallway, or do you walk past as if they're invisible? Do you thank the IT support person who resolved your computer issue, or do you treat them like a vending machine dispensing a solution? Do you engage the executive assistant with the same respect you show their executive, or does your demeanor shift based on perceived status? These micro-interactions reveal your true character, not the performance you give in front of senior leadership, but the authenticity (or lack thereof) you display when no one "important" is watching.

One of the most transformative habits you can develop as a leader is committing to know three personal facts about everyone you work with, not just your direct reports, but colleagues across departments, support staff, and even senior leaders. Not professional facts like "good at spreadsheets" or "handles conflict well," **but personal facts** like "do they have children? What do they do on weekends? Are they caring for aging parents? Training for a race? Renovating a house? Learning a new language?"

This practice fundamentally changes how you engage with people. When your knowledge of someone extends beyond what they can do for you professionally, you stop seeing them as a function and start seeing them as a whole person.

And here's what happens: Your conversations shift. Instead of transactional exchanges limited to work tasks, you build a genuine connection. "Hey John, how did your daughter's soccer tournament go this weekend?" "Sarah, did you finish that book you were reading?" "David, how's your mom doing after her surgery?"

These aren't trivial pleasantries; they're the threads that weave relational equity. When people know you care about their lives beyond their productivity, they trust you. When they trust you, they're more likely to be honest about struggles, more willing to go the extra mile, and more committed to the team's success. But even if none of that strategic benefit materialized, the practice would still be worth it, because seeing people fully is simply the right way to lead.

When you lead beyond your department, you don't just impact individuals; you shift organizational culture. Other leaders notice. Your direct reports observe how you treat people and begin to emulate them.

The receptionist you greeted warmly tells their colleagues, "That leader in Operations is really kind." The maintenance worker you helped feels valued and tells their team, "Not everyone here ignores us."

These stories can spread, and the acts can become contagious. **Over time, your reputation becomes, "That's a leader who genuinely cares about people."**

And here's the strategic benefit that often goes unspoken: When you need something, when your team faces a crisis, when you require urgent support from another department, when you're advocating for resources, the relational equity you've built across the organization becomes currency. People go the extra mile for leaders they respect. They prioritize requests from leaders who have treated them with dignity. They speak favorably of leaders who have consistently demonstrated servant leadership rather than self-promotion.

But even if none of that strategic benefit materialized, the practice would still be worth it, because leadership that transcends your department is leadership that reflects the kind of human connection we were created for.

It says, "You matter because you were created for more, not because of your utility to me."

It models a way of being in the world that prioritizes dignity over hierarchy, service over status, and genuine relationships over transactional interaction.

Chapter 12:

Communication and Connection

Leadership Rule # 29 - "Communication is the key that opens the door to relational equity..."

We just concluded Chapter 11 on relational equity and how it can become currency to advance the business. When we communicate effectively, we build trust, foster collaboration, and create a sense of belonging. According to the Harvard Business Review, companies with effective communication are more likely to have lower employee turnover. By investing in open, honest, and transparent communication, we can unlock the full potential of our relationships and create a culture of mutual respect, empathy, and understanding.

Effective leadership is rooted in empathy, intentionality, and the ability to truly know your people. Leaders who invest in building relational equity through consistent communication create trust and influence, thereby strengthening workplace relationships and driving performance. Simple acts, like greeting employees or acknowledging contributions at every level, compound into a culture of respect, gratitude, and psychological safety. This human-centered approach not only fosters creativity and resilience but also yields measurable outcomes, including higher engagement, lower turnover, and improved ROI. Ultimately, processes provide structure, but it is the leader's care, awareness, and purposeful connection with their team that enables lasting success.

Even in times of conflict, effective communication requires leaders to master specific techniques that transform tense moments into opportunities for resolution and growth. While we'll explore conflict resolution as a standalone competency in Chapter 22, it's essential to understand here how communication and conflict resolution work together. Active listening without making assumptions or getting defensive, simply saying "Tell me more" until the person's entire viewpoint is expressed, is a major strategy for de-escalation. Leaders should also modulate their voice to remain calm and even-toned, which significantly reduces the intensity of confrontation and helps soothe the other person. Finding common ground by identifying shared interests or goals shifts the focus from what divides people to what unites them, reminding everyone of the organization's broader goals and shared values, thereby reducing tension and fostering a spirit of teamwork.

Additionally, taking a brief pause when conversations become too heated gives everyone time to cool down and reflect, often leading to a more rational and solution-oriented approach when the conversation resumes. Leaders must also distinguish between assertive communication, expressing needs clearly and respectfully, and aggressive communication, which escalates conflict through blame, raised voices, or dismissive language.

After a conflict occurs, repair conversations are essential. Leaders should acknowledge harm done, take responsibility where appropriate, and work collaboratively to restore trust and relational equity within the team.

These communication strategies lay the groundwork for the deeper conflict-management framework we'll examine in Chapter 22.

Studies show that poor communication costs companies significantly, while effective communication boosts productivity and engagement. For example, employees spend nearly 88% of their workweek communicating, and strong communication reduces missed deadlines and stress.

Leadership Rule #533 "It's healthy to learn to listen so that we can listen to learn..."

When a leader learns to listen, they move beyond simply hearing words and instead pay attention to the emotions, intentions, and perspectives behind them. This kind of listening communicates respect and validation, showing team members that their voices matter. By practicing attentive listening, leaders build trust and relational equity, thereby creating an environment in which people feel safe to share ideas, concerns, and feedback. In turn, this strengthens the leader-team bond, laying the foundation for collaboration and growth.

But listening is not the end goal. It is the gateway to learning. When leaders listen to learn, they open themselves to new insights, diverse viewpoints, and innovative solutions that they might not have discovered on their own. This humility allows them to adapt, make better decisions, and empower others to contribute meaningfully. In practice, it means a leader doesn't just acknowledge input but actively integrates it into action, showing that listening leads to tangible outcomes. By combining the discipline of listening with the curiosity of learning, leaders cultivate a culture of growth where both individuals and the organization thrive.

However, even the most attentive listening can fail if leaders don't account for the perception gap, the distance between what someone intends to communicate and what the recipient hears. Effective listening requires recognizing that we don't hear words objectively. We filter them through our own experiences, biases, assumptions, and current emotional state. A team member might say, "I'm concerned about the timeline," and depending on our filters, we might hear criticism of our planning, anxiety about their workload, or a genuine attempt to problem-solve. What we perceive shapes how we respond, and if our perception is off, our response will miss the mark entirely.

This is why listening to learn demands more than passive reception; it requires active confirmation of understanding. Great leaders don't assume they've understood; they verify it.

After someone speaks, the listener reflects on what they heard: "What I'm hearing is that you're worried the timeline doesn't account for potential delays in permits. Is that accurate?"

This simple practice closes the perception gap by giving the speaker a chance to clarify, correct, or confirm. It signals humility, "I might not have heard you correctly," and respect, "Your actual meaning matters more than my interpretation."

Leaders must also recognize that their own responses are filtered through the listener's perception. You might offer what you intend as supportive feedback, but if the employee filters it through past experiences with harsh criticism, they may perceive condemnation rather than encouragement.

This is why effective communicators explicitly state their intent: "I'm sharing this because I see potential in you and want to help you grow, not because I'm disappointed."

By making your intent transparent, you reduce the risk of misinterpretation and help others receive your message as intended.

The goal isn't just to listen. It's to ensure that what you heard matches what was said. Misinterpretation is one of the greatest hindrances to effective communication, and it thrives in environments where leaders assume understanding rather than confirm it. When you commit to closing the perception gap, you transform listening from a passive act into an active, collaborative process that builds trust, prevents conflict, and unlocks the kind of honest dialogue where real learning happens.

Composer and conductor Gustav Mahler was known for an unconventional rehearsal technique: he periodically required orchestra members to leave their positions and sit in the audience, listening to the music from the audience's perspective. This forced musicians to hear how their individual contributions blended into the collective sound, something impossible to perceive accurately while playing. Violinists observed that their section balanced with the brass from row ten. Percussionists realized how their dynamics shaped emotional impact from the balcony. When they returned to their instruments, they played differently because they understood the experience they were creating, not just the notes they were executing.

Leaders must adopt the same discipline. Your perspective from your organizational position is necessarily limited. You hear the "music" of your leadership from the podium, but your team experiences it from the audience. If you never deliberately shift your frame of reference, never shadow your team, never solicit honest feedback about how your decisions land, never ask "How does this feel from where you sit?"—

you'll lead based on assumptions that may be completely disconnected from reality.

Changing perspectives changes leaders. When you experience your organization from where your people stand, you see blind spots, hear miscommunications, and feel friction points that were invisible from your vantage point. This isn't about doubting every decision or seeking constant validation. It's about recognizing that effective leadership requires epistemological humility. You don't know what you don't know until you change where you're standing.

Remember: Communication isn't what you say or what you hear; it's what's mutually understood. And mutual understanding only comes when leaders have the humility to verify, the curiosity to explore, and the discipline to listen beyond their own filters.

Cross-Cultural Communication: A Practical Framework

Working with people from different cultures isn't just about being "nice" or "politically correct." It's about recognizing that the way you communicate is shaped by where you grew up. For example, people from diverse cultures display different listening preferences. Germans, for example, favor an action-oriented approach, asking many questions and displaying keen curiosity. In contrast, the Japanese display an indirect approach, not directly inquiring but inferring from received cues. Americans, in contrast, focus on the time they are spending listening and conversing.

And here's the thing. Your way isn't the "right" way. It's just your way. Leading across cultures requires understanding that communication styles aren't preferences; they're deeply embedded in cultural programming.

Here are five steps on how to navigate:

Step 1: Know Your Own Communication Style First

Before you can navigate different communication styles effectively, you need to understand your default approach. **Take a moment to honestly assess how you naturally communicate**:

- **Are you direct or indirect?** When something won't work, do you say it plainly, or do you soften the message with phrases like "that could be challenging"?

- **Do you spell everything out or hint at meaning?** Some people provide explicit instructions while others drop subtle cues and expect team members to read between the lines.

- **Do you prioritize business or connections first?** Do you dive straight into the agenda, or do you need to build rapport before discussing work?

- **How comfortable are you with silence?** When conversation pauses, do you rush to fill the space, or can you sit comfortably in the quiet?

Your communication style isn't inherently superior or inferior to anyone else's. It's simply your starting point. Understanding your defaults helps you adapt intentionally rather than unconsciously impose your preferences on others.

Step 2: Learn How Your Team Actually Communicates

Different cultures operate by fundamentally different communication rules. Without awareness of these differences, even well-intentioned leaders can damage relationships and undermine trust.

- **In East Asia** (China, Japan, Korea), communication tends to be indirect and context-dependent. Silence doesn't signal confusion; it indicates thoughtfulness and consideration. Publicly correcting someone or calling them out in front of others can cause them to lose face, potentially destroying trust. Feedback should be delivered privately and framed diplomatically.

- **In Latin America**, relationships precede transactions. People want to know you as a person before fully engaging professionally. Expressiveness and emotional communication aren't considered unprofessional; they're normal and expected. When timelines shift, it's often because relational harmony is valued over rigid adherence to schedules.

- **In the Middle East**, trust and hospitality aren't peripheral concerns; they're foundational. Faith is often integrated into daily life and conversation. Your personal reputation carries significant weight, and relationship-building must precede business collaboration.

- **In Sub-Saharan Africa**, community and collective identity are central. The concept of Ubuntu, "I am because we are," shapes how decisions are made and relationships are valued. Storytelling often resonates more powerfully than data presentations, and decisions typically involve collective input rather than unilateral directives.

- **In South Asia** (India, Pakistan, Bangladesh), communication is frequently indirect to maintain harmony and preserve relationships. Family obligations take priority, and resourcefulness in challenging circumstances is highly valued.

The fundamental truth: what feels "normal" to you might come across as rude, cold, or disrespectful in another cultural context. Cultural awareness isn't a bonus skill for global leaders; it's a baseline requirement for effectiveness.

Step 3: Establish Communication Norms Together

Don't assume everyone shares the same expectations. Have explicit conversations with your team about how you communicate. **Consider asking:**

- "Do you prefer immediate feedback, or would you rather discuss it privately at a later time?"

- "When I ask if anyone has concerns in a meeting, do you actually feel comfortable speaking up in front of the group?"

- "What does 'urgent' mean to you? Same day, same hour, or something else?"

- "If we disagree during a meeting, what's the most constructive way to address that?"

You're not creating rules to control people. You're building clarity, so no one has to guess your expectations or get hurt by preventable misunderstandings.

Step 4: Adapt Your Style Contextually

The most effective leaders know how to adjust their communication style based on their audience. This isn't being inauthentic; it's being responsive and respectful.

- With a German team, be direct and structured. Document decisions thoroughly. Stick to the agenda. Efficiency demonstrates respect.

- With a Brazilian team, begin meetings with personal check-ins. Create space for emotional expression. Understand that timelines may be more flexible as relationships take precedence.

- With a Japanese team, get comfortable with silence. Use softer, more indirect language. Follow up in writing to ensure alignment and give people time to process.

- With a Nigerian team, embrace storytelling as a communication tool. Show respect for community values. Invest genuine time in building relationships beyond transactional interactions.

These are cultural tendencies and generalizations, not rigid rules that apply to every individual. Not every German is hyper-punctual, and not every Brazilian is highly expressive. But understanding these patterns provides a framework for thoughtfully adapting your approach.

This kind of flexibility isn't fake; it's a superpower that makes you fluent in different communication languages.

Step 5: When You're Uncertain, Ask

If you don't know how to communicate respectfully in someone's cultural context, ask them directly. It's far better than assuming and getting it wrong.

Try questions like:

- "In your culture, how do people typically show respect?"

- "What's the most effective way for me to give you constructive feedback?"

- "Is my communication style working for you, or should I adjust my approach?"

Curiosity and humility signal respect. People generally appreciate when leaders acknowledge what they don't know and ask to learn, rather than blundering forward with assumptions.

But wait, what about emojis?

Modern workplace communication increasingly occurs through digital channels, including Slack, Microsoft Teams, email, and text messages, and with this shift comes a new visual language, like emojis.

For leaders unfamiliar with, or dismissive of, this trend, understanding emoji usage isn't about being "cool" or "hip." It's about communicating effectively with a multigenerational workforce. Emoji usage in professional settings has surged in recent years.

Microsoft reported that emoji reactions in Teams increased by more than 1100% between 2020 and 2021, while Slack data indicate that workplaces have created more than 26 million custom emojis (Microsoft, 2021; Slack Technologies, 2023). Millennials and Gen Z increasingly use emojis professionally to convey tone (something notoriously difficult in text), soften direct feedback, express appreciation quickly, or clarify intent. A simple "Can we talk?" might read as ominous, but "Can we talk? 😊 " signals that the conversation isn't punitive. A "Great work on the report 👏 " adds warmth that plain text lacks.

Research indicates that 91% of emoji users report that emojis make it easier to express themselves. Millennials and

Gen Z use emojis professionally to convey tone (something notoriously difficult in text), soften direct feedback, express appreciation quickly, or clarify intent. A simple "Can we talk?" might read as ominous, but "Can we talk? 😊 " signals that the conversation isn't punitive. A "Great work on the report 👏 " adds warmth that plain text lacks.

However, emojis carry a significant risk of misinterpretation, especially across cultures and generations.

The 👍 (thumbs up) emoji is seen as a positive affirmation by older generations, but can be read as passive-aggressive or dismissive **by** Gen Z.

The 🙂 (slightly smiling face) is often interpreted by younger workers as sarcastic or insincere.

Professional norms vary. What's acceptable in Slack may not be appropriate in external client emails. Cultural meanings differ. Gestures that are positive in Western contexts may be offensive elsewhere. Leaders don't need to become emoji experts, but they do need to be aware.

Here are three ways to navigate this landscape:

1.   **Observe before adopting:** Notice how your team uses emojis in digital communication. What is the frequency? Which ones appear most often? Match their communication style to build rapport.

2.   **When in doubt, ask:** If you receive a message with an emoji you don't understand, simply ask: "Just want to make sure I'm reading your tone correctly, what did you mean by [emoji]?" This model of humility prevents misunderstandings.

3.   **Establish team norms:** Have explicit conversations about digital communication expectations. Some teams may prefer emoji-free professional communication; others may embrace it. Clarity prevents confusion.

The principle remains the same one we've emphasized throughout this book: effective communication requires meeting people where they are, not demanding they adapt entirely to your preferences. If your team communicates with emojis and you refuse to learn this language, you're creating an unnecessary barrier.

You don't have to love it; you just must care enough about the connection to make the effort. As one Gen Z employee told her Boomer manager who complained about emojis in Slack: "You learned Excel when computers became essential for your job. We're just asking you to learn a few pictures so we can communicate better together."

For a comprehensive field guide on cross-cultural communication strategies, see Appendix A at the end of this book.

Chapter 13:

Creating Meaningful Experiences

**Leadership Rule #106 - "Meaningful Moments are >
Meetings and Messages..."**

Now, this isn't meant to downplay team meetings, but
rather to call for greater interpersonal engagement. As
leaders, we often overlook the significance of everyday
interactions, dismissing them as mundane or routine.
However, it's precisely these moments that hold the greatest
potential for growth, connection, and impact. What
determines something as meaningful in the professional
world? Is it the interaction itself, or how we view the
interaction? The answer lies in our perspective. When we
approach each encounter with intention, empathy, and
curiosity, we transform the ordinary into extraordinary. By
doing so, we create opportunities for personal, professional,
and organizational growth.

If not careful, leaders can avoid memorable moments
because they become consumed by structure, efficiency, and
the formalities of leadership. Aspects such as meetings,
reports, and deadlines. In this mindset, everyday interactions
can feel too small or insignificant to warrant attention, so
they're dismissed as routine.

Yet, this avoidance stems from a misconception: Only big initiatives or formal gatherings drive impact. It is the casual hallway conversation, the quick "thank you," or the genuine check-in that builds trust and connection.

By overlooking these moments, leaders unintentionally miss opportunities to strengthen relationships and inspire growth.

In polychronic cultures, such as those in much of Latin America, Africa, and the Middle East, this principle is already embedded in daily life. Business happens over extended meals; relationships deepen through unhurried conversation, and the 'inefficient' time spent connecting is the most important work.

Western monochronic cultures often need to learn what polychronic cultures already know: Slowing down to connect isn't a distraction from work; it is the work.

So, what should be the goal for all? It's not just about making the interaction meaningful for the other person or us. It's about crafting an experience that resonates with both parties. As leaders, our aim should be to foster connections that inspire, motivate, and uplift. We must recognize that every interaction is an opportunity to build trust, share knowledge, and advance progress. By treating each encounter as meaningful, we not only enhance our leadership but also foster a culture of collaboration, innovation, and excellence. Ultimately, it's the accumulation of these meaningful moments that defines our legacy as leaders. By embracing this mindset, we can transform our day-to-day work experiences into a journey of growth, discovery, and purpose.

Priya, the department head, was setting up for the monthly team meeting when her director, Robert, stopped by early. "Big agenda today?" he asked, noticing the packed PowerPoint deck on her screen.

"Twenty slides," Priya said proudly. "KPIs, new initiatives, process updates, compliance reminders, everything they need to know."

Robert glanced around the empty conference room. "How long will that take?"

"Probably ninety minutes, but it's all important."

Robert pulled up a chair. "Can I share something I've learned? Last month, I sat in the back during one of these meetings. By slide ten, half the room was checking their phones. By slide fifteen, eyes were glazed over. The information was important, but the delivery lost them."

Priya looked deflated. "So, what should I do?"

"You're already thinking like a leader by wanting to keep everyone informed," Robert said. "But here's the question: how can we create moments that people remember, instead of meetings they just endure? What if you covered the five most critical points in twenty minutes, then spent the rest of the time in small groups, letting them discuss how these changes affect their actual work? That's where real connection happens, not in the slides, but in the conversation."

Priya nodded slowly. "So meaningful moments matter more than covering everything."

"Exactly," Robert said. "That's the kind of thinking that makes great leaders. I'm glad you're focused on that."

Leadership Rule #13 - "Create the space your team needs, not the one YOU want..."

Effective communication and conflict resolution in the workplace begin with humility and patience. Leaders who listen actively, ask thoughtful questions, and take accountability for their actions create a safe and respectful environment for open dialogue. In this space, individuals feel empowered to share their perspectives, and collaboration thrives. By prioritizing understanding over being understood, leaders can resolve conflicts efficiently and find solutions that benefit the organization. Ultimately, humility and patience are the catalysts for effective communication.

Leaders in any field often design environments based on their own preferences, but true effectiveness comes from shaping spaces around the needs of the people doing the work. In marketing and advertising, this means recognizing that creatives, analysts, and strategists may thrive in different conditions. For example, a copywriter may need quiet time to ideate, while a social media strategist may need collaborative brainstorming sessions. By creating the space your team needs, whether that's flexibility, psychological safety, or room for experimentation, leaders unlock innovation and prevent burnout.

This principle isn't limited to marketing. It applies universally.

Teachers who adapt classrooms to students' learning styles, coaches who tailor training to athletes' strengths, or managers in tech who build workflows around engineers' problem-solving habits.

In some cases, the student can be the teacher, and leaders would do well to recognize and learn from their team members' insights and experiences. To achieve this, leaders must keep the business needs central and remove emotions from the equation. By doing so, they can address conflicts and communication breakdowns objectively, focusing on finding solutions that drive results. When leaders take ownership of their actions and decisions, they demonstrate accountability and set a powerful example for their teams. By embracing humility, patience, and accountability, leaders can create a culture of effective communication, collaboration, and mutual respect.

Effective leadership is not about control or imposing one's own style, but about cultivating conditions where people feel valued, respected, and empowered.

Whether it's through designing the right environment or practicing humility in communication, the outcome is the same: Stronger relationships, healthier conflict resolution, and organizational success are built on trust and mutual respect.

Maybe you are reading this and are managing your first significant team or stepping into a director role, and you've finally got some actual influence over how things run. The temptation is to design everything around what worked for you when you were coming up, open-plan offices because you thrived on ambient energy, weekly stand-ups because you like accountability, or direct communication. After all, you hate ambiguity.

But intentional leadership asks a harder question: "What does this team need to perform at its best?"

The answer might surprise you. Your top performer might be someone who needs headphones and minimal interruptions to hit their stride. Your most innovative thinker might need permission to work remotely three days a week because their commute drains their creative bandwidth. Creating the space your team needs requires you to set aside your ego and observe what's working and what's quietly breaking people.

From a psychological standpoint, this principle taps into a fundamental aspect of human motivation and performance. Research in organizational psychology consistently shows that autonomy, mastery, and purpose drive engagement far more effectively than rigid structures imposed from above. When leaders create environments tailored to how people work best, they're signaling trust and respect, two foundational elements of psychological safety. And psychological safety isn't just a feel-good concept; it's directly correlated with higher performance, lower turnover, and better problem-solving. Teams that feel safe taking risks, voicing concerns, and admitting mistakes without fear of punishment outperform teams operating under surveillance and micromanagement every single time. So, when you create the space your team needs, rather than the one that makes you comfortable, you're not being a pushover. You're exercising wisdom. You're removing the friction that prevents people from doing their best work.

The uncomfortable truth is that many leaders resist this approach because it requires them to relinquish control and confront their own insecurities. If your team doesn't need the same structure you needed to succeed, does that mean your way wasn't the "right" way? If someone thrives under conditions that would have made you miserable, what does that say about your leadership philosophy? These questions can feel threatening, but they're liberating. Effective leadership isn't about cloning yourself or validating your own journey; it's about recognizing that the people you're leading are different from you, and that difference is a strength, not a problem to solve. The moment you stop trying to make your team fit your mold and start building around their actual needs, you'll see what's been possible all along. That's when innovation happens. That's when trust deepens. That's when people stop counting down to Friday and start showing up because they genuinely want to contribute to something meaningful.

To be clear: The business needs remain non-negotiable. Results matter, deadlines exist, and organizational goals must be met. But creating the space your team needs isn't about abandoning those objectives; it's about recognizing that there are multiple paths to achieving them, and the most sustainable path is one that honors both the mission of the business and the humanity of the people driving it forward.

Chapter 14:

Coaching, Mentoring, and Managing

Leadership Rule #114 - "Coaches, Mentors, and Managers..." Pt 1

A coach focuses on improving performance; a mentor fosters personal growth, and a manager drives organizational objectives. While these roles may overlap, their goals are unique. Understanding when and how to embody each role isn't just a leadership strategy; it's a response to a fundamental human need. Every person you lead has an innate desire to grow, improve, and become more capable than they were yesterday. This isn't a cultural construct or a professional expectation; it's wired into our neurological architecture. When we learn something new, our brains form new neural pathways and strengthen existing connections through a process called neuroplasticity. This biological reward system releases dopamine when we experience progress, creating a natural drive toward mastery and development. As leaders, we aren't creating this desire in our people; we're either nurturing it or malnourishing it.

Coaches aim to enhance skills; mentors seek to develop the whole person, and managers prioritize achieving business outcomes. Effective leaders recognize when to wear each hat, tailoring their approach to meet their team members' needs.

But here's what often goes unspoken: People don't just want to be managed. They require coaching and mentoring because these relationships satisfy a deeply human need.

From infancy, we're designed to learn through observation, guidance, and feedback. Children instinctively look to adults for modeling behavior and receiving correction. As we mature, this need doesn't disappear; it evolves. Adults still seek guidance, validation, and constructive challenges, not because they're weak or dependent, but because growth requires an external perspective.

You might be reading this book seeking the same thing. We have blind spots that we cannot see on our own. We develop habits that limit us without realizing it. A coach helps us see what we're doing; a mentor helps us see who we're becoming. Without these roles actively present in our lives, we plateau, not because we lack ambition, but because we lack relational scaffolding, which helps us reach the next level.

This dynamic reflects our need for what psychologists call "secure base leadership," a concept rooted in attachment theory. Just as children explore the world more confidently when they know they have a safe base to return to, adults perform at higher levels when they know someone is investing in their development and success. The presence of a coach, mentor, or manager who genuinely cares creates psychological safety, which research shows is the number one predictor of high-performing teams. When people feel seen, supported, and challenged appropriately, their brains operate in a state conducive to learning and risk-taking. Conversely, when they feel isolated, unsupported, or micromanaged without developmental investment, their brains trigger threat responses that inhibit creativity, problem-solving, and collaboration. This is why the best leaders don't just "get results." They create environments that activate people's neurological wiring for growth rather than suppress it.

Additionally, the human brain is socially designed. Neuroscience research indicates that mirror neuron systems enable learning from observation, and the prefrontal cortex helps integrate feedback and adjust behavior accordingly. This means we are literally built to be coached and mentored; our brains expect it. When leaders fail to provide coaching or mentorship, they're not just missing a management opportunity; they're neglecting a biological need. People who lack developmental guidance often experience stagnation, disengagement, and even burnout, not because the work is too hard, but because they're working without the relational input their brains require to make sense of their experiences and continue growing.

Effective leaders understand this and deliberately create pathways for feedback, development, and growth conversations. They recognize that while everyone wants autonomy, no one thrives in isolation. The sweet spot is guided by autonomy and the freedom to operate within a structure that provides the support needed to excel through coaching, mentoring, and clear management.

For example, a physician leading a surgical department must constantly shift between the roles of coach, mentor, and manager. As a coach, the leader provides real-time feedback to residents during surgical training, helping them refine technical skills and improve precision. This coaching ensures consistent quality of care and reduces medical errors, directly impacting patient safety and the hospital's reputation. As a mentor, the leader invests in the personal development of younger doctors outside the operating room, guiding them through career choices, work-life balance, and resilience in a demanding profession.

This mentorship fosters loyalty and reduces turnover, thereby saving the hospital substantial costs in recruitment and training. Finally, as a manager, the leader oversees budgets, staffing schedules, and compliance with healthcare regulations. By aligning team performance with organizational objectives, they ensure efficiency, profitability, and accreditation of success.

Mayo Clinic, a U.S.-based medical center, is widely recognized for its values-based leadership model, which emphasizes servant leadership and adaptability. Leaders are trained to act as coaches by giving real-time feedback to medical staff, ensuring precision, and reducing errors. They serve as mentors by fostering personal growth, resilience, and career development among physicians and nurses. As managers, they align departmental performance with organizational goals, including efficiency, compliance, and patient-centered care. This approach has led to higher patient satisfaction scores, stronger employee engagement, and improved operational efficiency, all of which reinforce Mayo's reputation as one of the world's leading healthcare institutions.

The principles of coaching, mentoring, and managing aren't reserved for those with impressive titles on business cards. Whether you're a C-Suite executive, Senior Director, Director, Manager, Supervisor, Team Lead, or individual contributor with informal influence, the fundamentals remain the same: emotional intelligence, effective communication, and conflict resolution are universal. What changes as you move up the organizational chart isn't the need for these competencies. It's the scale of impact and the complexity of application. A CEO who lacks emotional intelligence creates cultural dysfunction that cascades through thousands of employees. At the same time, a supervisor who avoids conflict allows toxicity to destroy the morale of their immediate team. The principles don't change; the consequences simply amplify or concentrate differently depending on the scope of influence. A VP who lacks self-awareness is as dangerous as a supervisor who lacks self-awareness; the VP simply harms more people more quickly.

Consider how leadership shows up at every level. The CEO coaches their executive team through strategic decisions and manages organizational vision, yet when they communicate ineffectively, confusion cascades through every level. The director translates executive vision into departmental reality by coaching managers and mentoring high-potential contributors; however, without conflict-resolution skills, they allow interpersonal tensions to fester, leading to stalled projects and talented people leaving. The manager holds perhaps the most challenging role: direct influence over people performing daily work, providing real-time feedback that shapes performance, and managing the operational realities that keep the organization functioning. Research consistently shows that people don't leave companies; they leave managers, not because managers are uniquely flawed, but because this is where leadership is felt most immediately. Even Team Leads, without formal authority, shape team culture through their emotional intelligence, communication style, and approach to conflict.

Leadership is leadership. In contrast, titles describe scope, not substance.

If you're reading this thinking, *"I'm just a supervisor, this doesn't fully apply to me,"* you're sadly mistaken. You are shaping human lives every single day, and the people you lead will remember how you made them feel long after they've forgotten the projects you completed together. If you're reading this as a C-Suite executive thinking, *"I'm beyond needing coaching on emotional intelligence,"* I would challenge you to question that thought. Your blind spots have organizational consequences, and the higher you rise, the fewer people have the courage to tell you the truth.

Every principle explored in this book, from tilling the soil of your own heart to cultivating harvests in others, from knowing your people to managing conflict with grace, applies to you, wherever you sit in the hierarchy. The question isn't whether these principles matter at your level; the question is whether you're humble enough to apply them.

Leadership Rule #115 - "Coaches, Mentors, and Managers..." Pt. 2

Is an effective leader someone who carries out just one of these functions, or all of them? Effective leaders wear multiple hats, seamlessly shifting between coaching, mentoring, and managing to drive success. Coaching develops skills, mentoring fosters growth, and managing achieves results.

Innate gift or learned behavior? This versatility is not an innate gift, but rather a learned behavior developed through practice, feedback, and self-awareness. Leaders who master this adaptability can build high-performing teams, drive business outcomes, and create a lasting impact. As leaders, we must be willing to evolve, learn, and grow alongside our teams. While some leaders may have a natural inclination toward one role, it's essential to develop the skills and competencies in the other two as well.

This logic applies well to the education sector, where leaders must continually adapt their roles to the needs of students, faculty, and the institution. A school principal or department head serves as a coach by helping teachers refine classroom strategies, offering feedback on lesson delivery, guiding students to improve academic performance and sharpen skills, and ensuring consistent quality in teaching and learning. The same leader becomes a mentor by supporting teachers in career development, encouraging students to explore their passions, and guiding staff through challenges such as burnout and work-life balance, thereby fostering loyalty, resilience, and long-term growth for both individuals and the institution. As a manager, the leader ensures classrooms, faculty, and resources are organized effectively, balancing schedules, setting priorities, and streamlining operations so that both teachers and students can thrive.

In the Middle East, this principle resonates deeply within cultural frameworks that have long valued the transmission of knowledge, the cultivation of character, and the stewardship of community. Consider the role of an educational leader in Dubai, Riyadh, or Amman, where schools serve not only as centers of academic learning but as guardians of cultural identity and social cohesion. Here, the distinction among coach, mentor, and manager assumes additional dimensions, shaped by values of respect, collective responsibility, and the preservation of tradition alongside progress. A principal, in this context, must coach teachers on pedagogy while remaining mindful of how teaching methods honor both modern educational standards and cultural expectations regarding discipline, gender dynamics, and family involvement. This is not simply about improving lesson plans; it's about equipping educators to navigate the delicate balance between innovation and tradition, ensuring that students excel academically without losing connection to their heritage.

As a mentor, the educational leader in the Middle East often bears responsibilities that extend beyond professional development to include moral and ethical guidance. In cultures where the concept of Tarbiyah, comprehensive education that includes moral and spiritual development, is central, mentorship involves helping teachers embody the values they are expected to instill in students: patience, humility, generosity, and a deep sense of duty to family and community. This mentorship may include conversations about how to remain resilient during Ramadan while maintaining teaching excellence, how to balance career ambitions with culturally prioritized family obligations, or how to support students navigating the pressures of high-stakes exams while staying grounded in their faith and identity. The mentor's role here is not transactional; it is relational and holistic, rooted in the understanding that a teacher's effectiveness is inseparable from their character and well-being.

As a manager, the leader must ensure that institutional goals are met while respecting the social fabric that holds the community together. In many Middle Eastern educational contexts, decisions are not made in isolation. They involve consultation with families, religious leaders, and governing bodies. Managing a school means balancing enrollment targets, budget constraints, and accreditation standards while honoring the trust parents place in the institution, viewing education as a sacred responsibility. It entails scheduling around prayer times, accommodating gender-specific needs when culturally appropriate, and fostering an environment in which both faculty and students feel their values are respected rather than compromised. The effective leader in this context understands that managing is not about imposing systems but about creating structures that allow people to flourish within their cultural and spiritual frameworks.

When these three roles, coach, mentor, and manager, are practiced with cultural intelligence and genuine respect, the result is an institution that not only achieves academic excellence but also strengthens the moral and social fabric of the community it serves.

Chapter 15:

Understanding Individual Strengths

Leadership Rule #36 - "Don't expect to get apples from an orange tree..."

Building on the "Know Your People" principle from Chapter 9 and the "People Over Process" framework from Chapter 10, **this leadership rule reflects a core principle of social psychology:** Realistic expectations are grounded in identity and capacity.

People bring unique traits, experiences, and limitations to any organization. Expecting someone to deliver results outside their natural strengths or current development stage leads to frustration, conflict, and disengagement. Social psychology emphasizes role congruence. When individuals are placed in roles that align with their abilities, they perform better, feel more satisfied, and contribute more meaningfully.

For effective leadership, this means recognizing that each team member has distinct skills and motivations. Success comes from leveraging those differences rather than forcing uniformity. **Leaders who understand this focus on strength-based leadership.** Assigning tasks that match people's competencies, providing coaching where growth is possible, and mentoring to expand potential over time. This approach fosters psychological safety, reduces stress, and builds trust, leading to higher engagement, stronger collaboration, and sustainable organizational success.

Achieving this requires collaboration between Recruiting, Human Resources, and Operations. Clear job descriptions set transparent expectations for both leaders and employees, ensuring alignment on responsibilities and outcomes while helping organizations recruit individuals whose skills match the role.

Organizational psychology has long recognized that people naturally fall into four working styles, often called the DISC (Dominance, Influence, Steadiness, Conscientiousness) model:

Doers (action-oriented, results-driven)

Talkers (relational, persuasive)

Listeners (supportive, steady)

Thinkers (analytical, detail-focused).

Most people are a combination of two styles, with one being dominant. Understanding your own blend reveals both your natural strengths and blind spots.

Effective leaders must:

- **Identify their top two styles -** This reveals their strengths and blind spots.

- **Identify these styles within their team.** This allows leaders to assign tasks that align with natural strengths rather than fighting how people are wired.

A Doer excels at launching initiatives but may struggle with patient follow-through. A Thinker ensures quality but may slow decision-making. A Talker rallies the team but may overlook details. A Listener maintains harmony but may avoid necessary conflict. Effective leaders don't expect everyone to operate the same way; they build teams where all four styles are represented and valued, creating a balance that drives sustainable success.

Leadership Rule #103 - "Teach Your Team to Catch Up, not Speed Up…"

Effective leaders recognize that people process information at varying speeds, and when team members fall behind, leaders often face a crucial decision.

Should they try to speed up the individual or help them catch up?

Speeding up entails accelerating an individual's pace to match others, which may not always be feasible or sustainable. In contrast, catching up involves providing targeted support to help individuals bridge the gap and meet expectations.

By focusing on catching up rather than accelerating, leaders can foster a more inclusive and supportive work environment. This approach acknowledges that each team member learns and processes information at their own pace. Rather than pressuring individuals to accelerate, leaders can offer resources, guidance, and feedback to help them catch up and succeed. By doing so, leaders can foster growth, build confidence, and drive collective success.

In many fast-paced tech companies, onboarding is often rushed to enable new hires to contribute immediately. Instead of providing structured training, mentorship, and gradual exposure to systems, leaders push employees to match the pace of seasoned staff.

The result is predictable: Higher error rates in code deployment, security oversights, and miscommunication across teams. These mistakes not only slow projects but also erode client trust and incur financial costs.

By contrast, organizations that invest in helping employees catch up, through extended onboarding programs, peer mentoring, and accessible resources, experience lower turnover, greater employee confidence, and faster long-term productivity gains. Tech giants such as Google and Microsoft have documented success with structured onboarding and continuous learning programs, showing that when leaders acknowledge diverse learning speeds, they build resilient teams that innovate more effectively.

This principle is powerfully illustrated in The Karate Kid (1984), a film that achieved global success across cultures and generations precisely because it captured a universal truth about learning and mentorship. When Daniel LaRusso arrives in California and asks Mr. Miyagi to teach him karate so he can defend himself against bullies, he expects immediate combat training. Instead, Miyagi assigns him seemingly menial tasks: waxing cars, sanding floors, and painting fences. Daniel becomes frustrated, convinced his teacher is wasting his time and exploiting his labor. He wants to speed up and learn the flashy moves immediately. But Miyagi isn't interested in speeding Daniel up; he's focused on helping him catch up to the foundational skills required for true mastery. Those repetitive motions, "wax on, wax off," "sand the floor," are building muscle memory, teaching defensive blocks, and instilling discipline that will serve Daniel for life, not just in the next fight.

It is my understanding that anyone watching this movie, anywhere in the world, can recognize the tension between the desire for immediate results and the need to lay proper foundations.

Mr. Miyagi understood what many leaders forget: Rushing someone through fundamentals doesn't create competence. It creates fragility.

When Daniel finally understands that he's been learning all along, not just performing chores, his confidence transforms. He catches up not by moving faster but by receiving targeted, patient instruction that helps him internalize skills at a sustainable pace. In the climactic tournament, Daniel doesn't win because he was rushed through training; he wins because Miyagi gave him time to absorb, practice, and truly own what he learned.

This is the essence of effective leadership: Recognizing that the fastest path to long-term success often requires slowing down initially to ensure everyone has the foundation they need. Leaders who pressure their teams to accelerate without ensuring understanding create a culture of anxiety and errors. Leaders who invest in helping people catch up, meeting them where they are, and building from there, create teams that perform with confidence, consistency, and enduring excellence.

Archilochus, an ancient Greek poet, once said that when we are under pressure, *"we don't rise to the occasion, we fall to our training."*

Leadership Rule #123 - "Manage the Person, Not the Profile..."

Understanding personality frameworks like DISC is valuable, but effective leaders recognize that people are more than their personality type. The danger of relying on personality assessments is that they can become boxes we place people in rather than tools we use to understand them. "Oh, she's a Thinker, that's why she's slow to decide." "He's a Talker, that's why he dominates meetings." These labels can serve as excuses that prevent us from addressing actual behaviors that require correction.

Here's the more nuanced truth: Personality influences behavior, but it doesn't excuse dysfunction. An extrovert who monopolizes every conversation isn't merely "being an extrovert." They fail to read the room and make space for others. An introvert who refuses to speak up in meetings when they have critical information isn't merely "being an introvert." They're failing to fulfill their responsibility to the team. A detail-oriented person who creates bottlenecks by overanalyzing every decision isn't merely "being conscientious." They're prioritizing perfection over progress, harming collaboration.

Your job as a leader isn't to accommodate every personality quirk uncritically. It's to help people understand how their natural tendencies impact others, and to coach them toward behaviors that serve the team without requiring them to become someone they're not.

This is the balance: Honoring who people are while holding them accountable for how they show up.

Extroverts process information externally. They think aloud, brainstorm verbally, and derive energy from group interaction. Introverts process internally, they think before speaking, prefer written communication, and need quiet to recharge. Most meetings are designed for extroverts, leaving introverts constantly at a disadvantage. The goal isn't to erase personality differences; it's to create systems where every personality can contribute at their best without disadvantaging others.

Chapter 16:

Hiring and Team Composition

Leadership Rule #108 - "We Need More Puzzle Pieces, Less Professionals..."

I mentioned the need for collaboration to ensure effective employee hiring. Does the quote above sound radical? In today's fast-paced business landscape, it's easy to get caught up in the idea that the most qualified candidate is always the best fit. We've been conditioned to believe that credentials, degrees, and certifications are the ultimate measures of a professional's worth.

Just as a puzzle requires diverse pieces to create a complete picture, a successful organization needs individuals with unique strengths, skills, and perspectives. Each puzzle piece represents a distinct talent, and when combined, they form a cohesive and powerful whole.

Think of it like a soccer team. You might have the most talented striker in the league, someone who can score from impossible angles and has a resume full of accolades. But if your midfielders can't distribute the ball effectively, if your defenders are constantly out of position, or if your goalkeeper lacks communication skills, that star striker becomes irrelevant. The goals don't come, and the team loses.

A championship soccer team isn't built by hiring eleven strikers. It's based on the premise that the center back's ability to read the game and make precise forward passes enables the attacking midfielder to create opportunities. The goalkeeper's vocal leadership and positioning give the defense confidence to press forward. The defensive midfielder who never scores goals might be the most valuable player because they recover possession and shield the backline, thereby allowing creative players to take risks. Every position impacts the overall goal differently, and each role, no matter how unglamorous, is essential to victory.

When hiring, the question shouldn't be "Who has the most impressive resume?" but rather "Who fits the position we need, complements the strengths and weaknesses of our existing team, and shares our values?"

A team full of "star players" who don't pass the ball, communicate, or trust one another will always lose to a cohesive unit where everyone understands their role and plays it with excellence.

The puzzle piece approach recognizes this truth: You don't need eleven strikers; you need the right mix of skills, perspectives, and heart postures working in harmony toward a common goal.

The truth is, being a viable candidate in the workplace is not just about having the right credentials; it's about embodying a heart posture that prioritizes values, experience, and a willingness to grow. By focusing on finding the right puzzle pieces, we can build a team that's greater than the sum of its parts. It's time to shift our mindset from seeking professionals with impressive credentials to finding individuals who embody the values, skills, and passion required to drive our organization forward. By doing so, we'll be better positioned to achieve our goals and succeed in an ever-evolving business landscape.

A study by Forbes found that 98% of employees would not work at a company whose values conflict with their own, highlighting the importance of values alignment for retention. These statistics reinforce the idea that credentials alone don't guarantee success. Just as puzzle pieces fit together to create a stronger, more cohesive team, diverse skills and values combine to create stronger, more cohesive teams. By painting a full picture of business needs and hiring for both competence and cultural alignment, leaders build organizations that are resilient, innovative, and better positioned to thrive in today's fast-paced environment.

Leadership Rule #202 - "Task Manager + People Leader = Effective Leader..."

Throughout my career, I have observed leaders who prioritize being overly social with their staff yet fail to follow through on executing tasks or challenging the team to address unmet needs. I have also observed leaders who, in their focus on tasks and forward planning, unintentionally overlook their staff's social, psychological, and professional needs. We need to be strong in both equally. We can't be great at managing tasks but not so great at managing people, or great at managing people, but not so great at managing tasks.

In healthcare facilities, some administrators prioritize overly relational interactions with staff, focusing on building morale and maintaining a supportive atmosphere, but fail to enforce critical operational standards, such as infection control protocols, HIPAA compliance, and staffing ratios. Others become so consumed with tasks like monitoring patient satisfaction scores, managing budgets, ensuring Joint Commission accreditation, and meeting state regulatory requirements that they unintentionally overlook the emotional exhaustion, burnout, and professional development needs of their clinical and administrative teams.

Effective leadership in healthcare administration requires strength in both areas. An administrator cannot succeed if they excel at managing operational metrics but neglect nurses experiencing compassion fatigue, front-desk staff overwhelmed by difficult patients, or physicians struggling with work-life balance. Nor can they thrive if they are great at supporting people emotionally but fail to maintain the compliance standards, safety protocols, and financial sustainability that keep the doors open.

True success comes from balancing operational excellence, regulatory compliance, and patient safety with the fostering of trust, recognition, and professional growth among staff.

This balance not only improves patient outcomes and reduces medical errors but also decreases staff turnover, enhances employee retention, and builds a resilient team capable of thriving in the high-pressure, emotionally demanding environment of healthcare. When administrators master this duality, they create facilities where people want to work and where patients seek to receive exceptional care. Being an effective leader requires a high social IQ, emotional IQ, and work efficiency IQ.

Here's a helpful hint to raise awareness: The key lies in understanding the above lies in our identity and in our understanding of it.

Chapter 17:

Team Dynamics and Unity

Leadership Rule #112 - "Alliances vs. Allegiances: Navigate Them Well..."

One of the most valuable attributes of an effective leader is their ability to assess and observe their team to ensure unity and prevent division. Understanding the difference between alliance and allegiance is essential for leaders managing team dynamics, especially when cliques begin to form. An alliance reflects a strategic partnership that can benefit the team, while allegiance signals personal loyalty that may lead to exclusivity and division.

Leaders must observe whether the relationship is collaborative or isolating and assess its impact on team cohesion. By identifying the underlying intent, leaders can either encourage productive alliances or redirect misplaced allegiances toward shared goals. This awareness helps maintain a healthy, inclusive team culture and prevents fragmentation.

Human beings are wired for connection; psychologists consistently point to "belonging" as a fundamental human need that shapes our identity and sense of security. We are made for the unity found in community (the group of like-minded people we associate with).

But here's the complication: Alongside that drive for connection lives something equally powerful, self-interest. The desire for recognition, influence, or personal advancement doesn't disappear just because someone joins a team. Within any workplace, these two forces coexist, sometimes harmoniously, sometimes in tension. Employees genuinely want to collaborate, but they're also protecting their own careers. Leaders champion unity while quietly guarding their authority. This isn't a character flaw; it's human nature. And pretending it doesn't exist won't make it go away.

The leader's responsibility is to observe what's happening, not what they wish were happening. Watch how people interact. Notice who gravitates toward whom and why. Are these connections building trust within the team, or are they creating invisible barriers that exclude others? Is ambition driving people toward collective achievement, or is it creating competition that undermines collaboration? The best leaders don't try to eliminate self-interest; they redirect it. They create environments where individual ambition and team success are complementary goals rather than opposing forces. This requires systems that reward transparency, celebrate shared victories over individual heroics, and make space for honest dialogue about competing priorities.

When leaders balance the psychology of connection with the reality of self-interest, they cultivate cultures where individuals thrive together. As we saw in Chapter 6, 70% of the variance in employee engagement stems from leadership behavior, which is why balancing connection with accountability is so important. Unity doesn't happen by accident. It's the result of leaders who pay attention, intervene when necessary, and intentionally design environments where people's natural drive for belonging and achievement can coexist without creating division.

Three encouragement keys when dealing with team dynamics:

1. Not all close relationships are harmful.

2. Encourage alliances that benefit the whole team.

3. Realign allegiances toward the team and mission.

Jason, the new associate, was grabbing coffee in the break room when he noticed his manager, Carla, observing the dynamics in the corner where several team members were gathered. After they left, Carla turned to him. "Did you notice anything just now?" Jason shrugged. "Just people taking a break."

"Look closer next time," Carla said. "That's the same group that always sits together. They don't invite anyone else, and when others approach, the conversation shifts. It's subtle, but it's creating division."

Jason frowned. "I thought team members becoming friends was a good thing?"

"Friendship is great," Carla said. "But when it becomes exclusive, when it creates an 'in-group' and an 'out-group,' it damages the whole team. I've seen three people request transfers in the last six months, and when I asked why, they all said they felt like outsiders."

"I had no idea," Jason admitted.

"That's okay, you're learning," Carla said. "The question of how we can help our people build genuine connections without creating cliques is critical. We want alliances that strengthen the team, not allegiances that fracture it. You're starting to see it now, and that's thinking like a leader. That awareness is exactly why I know you're ready for this role."

Over the following weeks, Jason implemented Carla's teachings. He began rotating seating in meetings, creating cross-functional project teams that mixed the usual groups, and privately coaching the clique members about inclusive behavior. The shifts were subtle but effective; within two months, the break room dynamics had changed, and no one else requested a transfer.

You cannot stop your employees from building relationships. In fact, you should encourage it. What needs to be constantly reiterated is the notion that the whole is greater than the sum of its parts. Making friends at work is great, but accomplishing the business's goals is what we signed up for.

One is required; the other is not. Both are necessary to cultivate a healthy, thriving work environment.

Consider how ant colonies achieve this. With no centralized command, no org chart, and no performance reviews, millions of ants coordinate flawlessly. Scouts discover resources and leave chemical trails for foragers. Foragers gather food and share it through trophallaxis (mouth-to-mouth feeding) with nursery workers who never leave the nest. Soldiers defend the perimeter so others can work without fear. Each ant performs its role not for recognition, but because the colony's survival ensures its own.

Bee hives operate similarly. A forager doesn't hoard the location of nectar-rich flowers; she performs a waggle dance to communicate coordinates to other bees. House bees don't compete to produce the most honey; they collectively transform nectar into sustenance for the entire hive. When winter comes, the bees that survive do so because thousands contributed their 1/12 teaspoon, creating collective abundance from individual sacrifice.

Human teams thrive under the same principles. The leader who sees themselves as the queen bee, entitled to deference, demanding loyalty, and consuming resources, misunderstands the metaphor entirely. The queen doesn't lead. She ensures continuity. The hive thrives because every member knows their role matters, contributes faithfully, and trusts that others are doing the same. When leaders shift from "what can my team do for me?" to "how do I create conditions where every person's contribution compounds into something greater?" that's when organizations transform from hierarchies into ecosystems.

Leadership Rule #4- "Leaders who are obsessed with themselves won't have any room to invest in their staff..."

Leaders obsessed with their own progression find it nearly impossible to genuinely celebrate their team's success. When your primary focus is climbing the next rung on your own ladder, everyone around you becomes either a tool to help you get there or an obstacle in your way. Neither perspective builds trust. Employees who work under self-absorbed leaders often feel like characters in someone else's career narrative, valued only for how they make the leader look, not for who they are or what they could become. This dynamic might initially present as confidence or ambition, but it doesn't take long for team members to recognize they're being used rather than developed.

Here's the paradox: The leaders most desperate to advance their own careers are often the ones who plateau earliest. Why? Because leadership at higher levels isn't measured by what you personally accomplish, it's measured by what you enable others to accomplish.

A self-focused approach stifles the very qualities organizations need most. Collaboration, creativity, innovation, and loyalty.

When your team senses that every project, every win, every initiative is ultimately about boosting your profile rather than genuinely solving problems or serving clients, they disengage. They do exactly what is required and nothing else. You get compliance, not commitment.

The leaders who progress, who build reputations that open doors and create opportunities, are the ones who invest in their people first. They understand that their team's success is their success, not in a transactional "you make me look good" sense, but in a genuine "your growth matters to me" sense.

These leaders ask questions like, "Who on my team is ready for more responsibility? Who needs coaching to overcome a specific challenge? Who has potential that's being overlooked? Where can I create pathways for development that didn't exist before?" This mindset shifts from "What can my team do for me?" to "What can I do to unlock what's possible in my team?"

This is what separates leaders who manage from leaders who transform.

Look at the evolution of leadership over the past century. Authoritarian, command-and-control models dominated early corporate America because they worked in stable, predictable environments where efficiency mattered more than innovation. But those models consistently failed to inspire loyalty, adaptability, or creative problem-solving. When industries shifted, when crises emerged, when markets evolved, the leaders stuck in self-focused hierarchical thinking couldn't pivot fast enough. The organizations that survived and thrived were led by people who had built strong, empowered teams capable of navigating complexity together. This wasn't a happy accident; it was a direct result of investing in people rather than hoarding control.

I've watched this play out at some point in my career. The leaders who lasted, who earned genuine respect, who were sought after for bigger roles, were never the ones obsessed with their own visibility. They were the ones who developed other leaders, who gave credit generously, who created opportunities for their teams to shine even when it meant stepping back.

I've also seen the opposite: Talented individuals promoted into leadership who couldn't let go of personal glory. They micromanaged, took credit for team wins, and viewed every success as validation of their own brilliance. Some got promoted once or twice more on the momentum of early results. Still, eventually, organizations figured out what their teams already knew: these leaders couldn't scale because they refused to share the spotlight.

Modern leadership is measured not by titles or tenure, but by your ability to create environments where people want to contribute to their best work. If you're fixated on your own progression, you'll miss the talent sitting right in front of you. You'll overlook the quiet performer who needs one conversation to unlock their potential. You'll dismiss the team member whose idea could solve the problem you've been stuck on for months. Self-obsessed leadership isn't just ethically questionable; it's strategically foolish. The leaders who embody the future of this profession understand that influence isn't about self-promotion. It's about cultivating cultures in which the collective strength of the team defines what's possible, and in which your legacy is measured not by the titles you held but by the leaders you developed.

Research published by the "Chief Talent Officer" highlights the hidden costs of leader-centric cultures. When organizations overemphasize individual leadership pipelines, they often neglect team development, leading to disengagement and stalled innovation. Shifting to team-focused strategies restores balance and drives sustainable growth.

Chapter 18:

Cultivating Growth and Potential

Leadership Rule #110 - "Don't wake them up, raise them up..."

In speaking with several leaders, I've learned that many don't know how to respond to the "dreamers" on their teams. It's important not to extinguish the flames of imagination by forcing reality checks. Instead, fan the fires of creativity and innovation by empowering your dreamers to soar. Don't wake them up. Raise them up to new heights, where their vision and passion can converge with practicality and wisdom.

Yet leaders must also recognize how ego and insecurity can quietly derail this process. When dreamers are overlooked because a leader feels threatened, or when their ideas are brushed aside as "too much," the entire team feels the ripple effect. Others grow hesitant; collaboration weakens, and innovation gets buried under doubt. Applying this rule helps leaders move beyond self-protection toward team progress, ensuring that visionaries are nurtured rather than suppressed.

By doing so, you'll unleash a powerhouse of potential that can transform your organization and change the world, while ensuring no one else feels overshadowed or inferior. This balance isn't always possible due to workplace restrictions, but when the opportunity arises, the effective leader must identify it and pursue it. Elevating people in this way, without letting ego or insecurity take root, is how teams grow stronger together.

Three ways to "Raise Up" your dreamers:

1. **Provide autonomy and ownership:** Give dreamers the freedom to pursue their ideas and passions, and the resources and support they need to succeed.

2. **Offer guidance and mentorship:** Pair dreamers with experienced mentors who can offer guidance, wisdom, and constructive feedback to help them refine their ideas and navigate challenges.

3. **Foster a culture of experimentation and learning:** Encourage dreamers to take calculated risks, experiment with new ideas, and learn from their failures. This will help them develop resilience, adaptability, and a growth mindset.

Adam Grant articulated this when he said, "If you want people to take risks and learn from failure, you need to create a culture where it's safe to fail."

Several years ago, a mid-level manager named Sophia noticed one of her team members, Daniel, was brimming with ideas for a new product line. His enthusiasm was contagious, but his boldness intimidated the rest of the team, who began to feel overshadowed. Meetings grew tense, with colleagues withdrawing rather than engaging. Sophia realized that if Daniel's energy wasn't managed carefully, the team dynamic would collapse.

Rather than silencing him, Sophia paired Daniel with a mentor from another department and assigned him a small pilot project to test his ideas. At the same time, she made space in team meetings for others to share their perspectives, ensuring Daniel's voice didn't dominate. Over time, Daniel's vision matured into a viable initiative, while the rest of the team regained confidence, knowing their contributions mattered. The project succeeded not because Daniel was "woken up" with reality checks, but because he was "raised up" in a way that allowed him to grow, without making others feel small. Sophia's leadership proved that nurturing visionaries while protecting team cohesion is the hallmark of an effective leader.

Waking dreamers up means forcing them back into rigid reality, while raising them up means empowering their vision and guiding it toward practical outcomes. Effective leaders channel imagination into innovation, allowing passion and practicality to converge for collective success.

Leadership Rule #33 - "Keep Growing Your Garden…"

Just like a garden requires careful tending to flourish, our unique journeys and assignments require intentional nurturing to reach their full potential. A farmer knows that weeds must be removed to prevent them from choking the harvest; fertilizer must be added to enrich the soil, and water must be provided consistently to sustain life.

In the same way, leaders must prune away distractions, enrich their minds with new knowledge, and nourish their spirit with purpose. When this care is given, both the field and the team grow strong and resilient, capable of withstanding droughts, storms, and changing seasons. The greatest yield comes not from neglect or chance, but from steady, intentional cultivation, producing a harvest that benefits many and leaves a lasting impact.

As we navigate today, let's focus on cultivating the soil of our hearts so that we may yield a bountiful harvest of impact and influence. The greatest contribution a leader can make is to do the necessary work within themselves to make these goals tangible to others.

This internal work, which I addressed in Chapter 5 as soul health, is not separate from leadership development. It is its foundation.

You cannot grow a garden you refuse to tend. The leader who neglects their own emotional wholeness, who ignores unresolved pain or unexamined motivations, is like a farmer scattering seeds on hardened ground. The seeds may land, but they won't take root. Throughout my career, I've witnessed leaders with impressive résumés and sharp minds fail to sustain impact because they never addressed what was happening beneath the surface. They accumulated credentials, climbed titles, and delivered results for a season, but their internal soil was depleted. Eventually, the harvest stopped. Not because they lacked talent, but because they lacked the soul health necessary to steward that talent over the long term.

Growing your garden means tending to your own heart first. It means the process of doing the difficult work of pulling weeds like bitterness, fear, and ego, enriching your spirit through reflection and rest, and watering your soul with relationships and practices that keep you grounded.

Here's the truth that ties everything together: The three pillars we explored in the Introduction, emotional intelligence, effective communication, and conflict resolution, are all fruit that grows from healthy soil. You can study techniques, memorize frameworks, and attend every leadership training available, but if your internal garden is neglected, those skills won't sustain. Emotional intelligence requires self-awareness, which comes only from tending to your heart. Effective communication flows from a soul that's addressed its own wounds and insecurities, allowing you to engage others without defensiveness or projection. Conflict resolution demands the inner stability to hold tension without collapsing into reactivity or control.

These aren't compartmentalized skills you bolt onto your leadership persona; they're the natural harvest of a soul that has been consistently and intentionally cultivated. When you grow your garden, you don't just improve yourself; you create the conditions for your entire team to flourish.

Chapter 19:

Building Your Team's Harvest

**Leadership Rule #104 - "Cultivating a Harvest is >
Building a Team..." Pt. 1**

Cultivating a harvest is more important than building a
team, because true leadership is not about assembling a
group of individuals but about nurturing a community of
people who have been empowered to grow, flourish, and
bear fruit. A harvest is not just a collection of individuals; it's
a vibrant, thriving ecosystem where each person's unique
gifts and talents are valued, multiplied, and released to make
a lasting impact.

In a community social work agency, a director faced high
turnover and burnout among caseworkers. Still, instead of
simply building a team by hiring more staff and assigning
caseloads, she shifted her focus to cultivating a harvest by
nurturing growth, resilience, and empowerment. Drawing on
Self-Determination Theory, she recognized that people thrive
when their needs for autonomy, competence, and relatedness
are met. Therefore, she granted caseworkers greater
decision-making authority, provided ongoing training, and
fostered peer support groups. This investment in the
ecosystem of growth, rather than just the team's structure, led

to higher job satisfaction, stronger emotional resilience, and deeper commitment to clients. Burnout rates dropped, and the agency saw improved client outcomes because workers felt valued and supported. By cultivating a harvest rather than merely building a team, the director fostered sustainable growth, resilience, and lasting impact for both her staff and the community they served.

There's a quote that says, *"You can count the number of seeds in an apple, but you cannot count the number of apples in a seed."*

As leaders, we often underestimate the ripple effect of our influence. Just as one seed can grow into countless apples, a single life touched by our effective leadership style can multiply into a harvest of transformed lives.

The mathematics of cultivation reveals a profound truth. That multiplication always outpaces addition.

Research from Gallup shows that employees who feel their development is being invested in are 3.5 times more likely to be engaged at work, and highly engaged teams show 21% greater profitability.

But here's what those numbers don't fully capture: The compounding effect over time. When you build a team, you're adding capacity. Hire five people, and you have five people's worth of output.

But when you cultivate a harvest, you're multiplying potential. Invest deeply in five people, and they grow into leaders who develop others, who develop others, who develop others, who develop others. Suddenly, your influence extends far beyond the people sitting in your direct reports meeting. It ripples through the organization and, eventually, into other organizations as those you cultivated assume leadership roles, carrying the seeds you planted.

I've witnessed this multiplication effect throughout my career. Early in my time in BPO, I worked under a leader who saw something in me I hadn't yet recognized in myself. He didn't just assign me tasks; he created opportunities for me to stretch into areas that terrified me. He assigned me projects that required me to develop skills I didn't have, and then coached me through the inevitable mistakes. When I succeeded, he celebrated publicly. When I failed, he debriefed privately and reframed failure as data, not defeat. Years later, when I moved into senior leadership roles myself, I found myself replicating that same approach with my own teams; not because I'd read it in a book, but because I'd experienced it. And now, the people I've mentored are doing the same with their teams. That one leader's decision to cultivate rather than simply manage created a harvest that can extend decades beyond his tenure and touch people he'll never meet.

That's the power of cultivation. It doesn't stop with you.

Contrast this with the transactional approach many leaders default to. They build teams like assembling machinery, filling roles, assigning tasks, and measuring output.

People become functionaries. You do this job, produce these results, and stay within these parameters.

There's no investment in growth, no consideration of potential, no long-term vision beyond immediate productivity. This approach might work for a season, especially in stable environments where tasks are repetitive and turnover is tolerable. But it's fundamentally unsustainable.

Research from the Work Institute shows that a lack of career development is the primary reason employees leave their jobs, accounting for 22% of all turnover. When people feel like cogs in a machine rather than seeds being cultivated, they disengage emotionally long before they physically leave. And when they do leave, they take with them not just their current productivity, but all the potential harvest they could have produced if someone had invested in their growth. The leader who merely builds teams finds themselves perpetually rebuilding, constantly replacing people, never experiencing the exponential return that comes from multiplication. They work harder but harvest less, wondering why their efforts never seem to compound into something greater.

Leadership Rule #105 - "Cultivating a Harvest is > Building a Team…" Pt. 2

To cultivate a fruitful harvest, we must first learn how to till the soil, be willing to get pricked, uproot, and make the soil fertile again.

• **Tilling the Soil** (Getting Through the Hardness of One's Heart): Heart reconstruction will be essential in this process, but it starts with us. Before we can help others recognize where they are, we must first recognize our own biases, limitations, and areas for growth. Be willing to confront and work on your own "hard parts." We can grow in this by learning to manage our emotions, empathize with others, and maintain a growth mindset.

• **Getting Pricked by Thorns** (Hurt by Those You Lead): As leaders, we're often encouraged to create safe spaces for open communication, feedback, and constructive criticism. **However, this openness comes with a risk.** The more we engage with others, the more vulnerable we become to being hurt by them. Every conversation, every piece of feedback, and every criticism carries the potential to pierce our defenses and touch our emotions. To navigate this vulnerability, we must develop a growth mindset that acknowledges the inevitability of setbacks and conflicts.

Openness increases connection and performance, but it also heightens exposure to social pain. Neuroscience shows that the brain processes social rejection using neural pathways similar to those for physical pain, which is why critical feedback can feel viscerally threatening and trigger defensive reactions. This "threat response" can narrow attention, reduce cognitive flexibility, and push leaders into fight–or–flight behaviors that undermine constructive dialogue. Recognizing this normal, human response is the first step to leading with steadiness under emotional pressure.

Engaging more deeply with others increases vulnerability because social evaluation activates the brain's threat systems, amplified by negativity bias and identity-protective cognition. A growth mindset, paired with emotional intelligence skills and psychologically safe norms, reframes setbacks as learning signals, converts criticism into actionable experiments, and preserves connection, allowing leaders to benefit from openness without being overwhelmed by it.

This process of tilling, pruning, and cultivating directly connects to the soul health we explored in Chapter 5. Remember Pete Scazzero's warning that "the darker side of leadership is that it can be a powerful catalyst for revealing the deepest, most hidden parts of our hearts."

Cultivation isn't just an agricultural metaphor. It's spiritual and emotional surgery.

When we till the hardened soil of our own hearts, we're doing the inner work that determines whether our leadership bears lasting fruit or withers under pressure.

Leaders who skip this step and focus only on external techniques discover, often painfully, that unexamined wounds and unhealed pain inevitably leak into their leadership. You cannot give what you don't possess. If your soul remains untended, cluttered with bitterness, driven by insecurity, or hardened by past hurts, you'll find yourself reacting rather than responding, defending rather than listening, and ultimately damaging the very people you're called to cultivate.

The willingness to be pricked by thorns is, paradoxically, what protects your team from your unprocessed pain. When leaders refuse to engage vulnerably out of fear of being hurt, they create defensive cultures where honest feedback becomes dangerous and psychological safety evaporates. But when you've done the soul work, when you've allowed God, a therapist, a mentor, or trusted accountability partners to expose and heal your own thorns, you develop the emotional capacity to receive correction without collapsing into shame or lashing out in anger.

This is the fruit of emotional intelligence we discussed in Chapter 3: Self-awareness that recognizes your triggers, self-regulation that manages your reactions, and empathy that allows you to hold space for others' perspectives even when they challenge your own. The leader who has been pricked and survived, who has allowed criticism to refine rather than define them, becomes safe for their team to approach them with truth. And truth-telling is the oxygen innovation requires.

Ultimately, cultivating a harvest demands that we embrace the uncomfortable reality that growth is always preceded by disruption. Tilling breaks up compacted soil. Pruning cuts away branches that feel productive but drain resources from deeper fruit. Uprooting pulls out what's familiar but toxic.

This isn't comfortable work. It's the kind of leadership development that requires what we discussed in Chapter 4 about mental and emotional wellbeing: The courage to admit "it's ok to not be ok," the humility to seek help before you break, and the wisdom to recognize that your capacity to cultivate others is directly proportional to your willingness to be cultivated yourself.

Leaders who refuse this process become the bottleneck in their own organizations, talented, hardworking, but ultimately unable to scale their impact because they've never allowed anyone to till the soil of their own hearts. But leaders who embrace cultivation, who stay in therapy, who remain in spiritual formation, who keep learning, who surround themselves with people who have permission to speak truth, these are the leaders whose influence multiplies exponentially, because they're not just building teams, they're cultivating ecosystems where everyone grows together.

Chapter 20:

The Leader's Identity

Leadership Rule #188 - "Leadership Anchored in Style, Not Emotion…"

Identity plays a significant role in leadership because it shapes how a leader perceives themselves and interacts with others. A strong sense of identity provides confidence, clarity, and consistency, qualities that help leaders establish trust and make sound decisions. When leaders understand who they are and what they stand for, they can align their management style with their values, thereby fostering authenticity and stability within their team.

What about people in leadership positions who struggle with insecurities or low self-esteem? This doesn't automatically disqualify them from becoming an effective leader, but it does present challenges. After all, we all face some form of misconception about ourselves. Insecure leaders may struggle with decision-making, overcompensate through control, or seek validation in unhealthy ways. However, with self-awareness and a commitment to growth, these individuals can develop confidence over time. Many successful leaders started with doubts but built resilience through experience, mentorship, and continuous learning.

The key is whether they are willing to address those insecurities and adopt a leadership style that prioritizes the team over personal fears.

Effective leaders need a defined management style because it provides structure, consistency, and clarity in decision-making. A management style acts as a guiding framework that aligns actions with organizational goals, fosters trust among team members, and ensures fairness in handling challenges. Without a clear approach, leadership can become unpredictable, making it harder for teams to understand expectations and maintain confidence in their leader's decisions. A well-developed style also helps leaders adapt to different situations while staying grounded in principles rather than impulses.

Conversely, when leadership decisions are driven primarily by emotions, outcomes can become inconsistent and potentially harmful to team morale and productivity. Emotions, while valuable for empathy and connection, are not always reliable for strategic thinking or conflict resolution. Leaders who lack a structured approach risk reacting impulsively, which can lead to favoritism, poor judgment, and instability within the organization. By establishing a management style, leaders create a balanced environment where emotional intelligence complements, rather than overrides, rational decision-making.

Here are the five most common leadership styles. Which would you say you are?

1. **Autocratic Leadership** - The leader makes decisions unilaterally with little input from team members.

2. **Democratic Leadership** - Decisions are made collaboratively, encouraging team participation and feedback.

3. **Transformational Leadership** - Focuses on inspiring and motivating employees to innovate and embrace change.

4. **Transactional Leadership** - Relies on structured tasks, clear rules, and rewards or penalties to achieve goals.

5. **Laissez-Faire Leadership** - Provides minimal direction, allowing team members significant autonomy in decision-making.

When a leader commits to a healthy management style, they are essentially committing to the well-being and success of their team. A structured, thoughtful approach ensures that decisions are fair, transparent, and aligned with shared goals, which builds trust and respect. This commitment signals to employees that their leader values stability and growth over impulsive reactions, creating an environment where people feel supported and empowered. In short, a healthy management style isn't just about managing tasks; it's about investing in people and fostering a culture where everyone can thrive.

The healthier a leader is, within their soul, the safer the team is around them.

Chapter 21:

Below the Surface: The Iceberg Model of Leadership

Leadership Rule #107 - "Effective Leaders are Scuba Divers, Not Snorkelers..."

When you look at your team, what do you see? Performance metrics, attendance records, meeting participation, work quality; these are the visible indicators, the tip of the iceberg. However, effective leaders recognize that what they observe accounts for only 10% of what drives their people. The remaining 90%, the beliefs, fears, traumas, past experiences, values, and unspoken motivations, lie hidden beneath the surface. Just as most of an iceberg's mass remains submerged and invisible, the majority of what drives human behavior in the workplace is concealed from view. Leadership isn't about managing what you see; it's about understanding what you don't.

Here's the tension: To lead effectively, you need to understand what's beneath the surface. But you're not a therapist, and the workplace isn't a confessional. So how do you access the "glacier" without crossing inappropriate boundaries? Relationship-building over time builds trust, granting access to deeper layers while always respecting privacy and professionalism.

Boundaries that should NOT be crossed:

- Prying into personal matters that don't impact work performance

- Forcing disclosure of private struggles (health issues, family problems, financial stress)

- Using personal information against someone in evaluations or decisions

- Creating dependency where employees feel obligated to share intimate details

- Becoming a personal counselor or attempting to "fix" someone's life

Here's the difference in practice:

When Sheila noticed her team member, Tom, becoming withdrawn and missing deadlines, she had a choice. She could have demanded to know what was "going on at home" (crossing a boundary).

Instead, she said, "Tom, I've noticed you seem stressed lately. I'm not asking you to share anything private, but I want you to know I'm here if work adjustments would help."

Tom eventually shared that his father was ill, and together they created a temporary, flexible schedule. Sheila accessed the glacier without prying; she created safety and let Tom decide what to share.

Appropriate Ways to Access the Glacier:

• **Build consistent, genuine relationships over time** - Regular check-ins, not just when problems arise.

• **Create psychological safety** - Show through actions that honesty won't be punished.

• **Ask open-ended, caring questions** - "How are you really doing?" "What's on your mind lately?" "What can I do to support you better?"

• **Observe patterns, then inquire with empathy** - "I've noticed you seem stressed lately. Is there anything affecting you that I should be aware of?"

• **Share appropriately about yourself** - Vulnerability invites vulnerability (within professional limits).

• **Respect when people aren't ready to share** - Trust is earned, not demanded.

Practical Application: The "Iceberg Check-In" Framework

When you observe a concerning behavior, pause and ask yourself:

1. What am I seeing? (Name the observable behavior)

2.   What might be beneath it? (Brainstorm 3-5 possible hidden drivers)

3.   What do I know about this person's context?

4.   How can I inquire with curiosity instead of judgment?

5.   What support can I offer if they share more?

By keeping an open mind and being curious about what's beneath surface behaviors, leaders build empathy and avoid rushing to judgment.

Your team is not a collection of tasks to be managed; they are complex human beings carrying unseen weight, unspoken dreams, and hidden struggles. The leader who sees only the tip of the iceberg will constantly be surprised, frustrated, and ineffective. But the leader who commits to understanding the glacier, with patience, respect, and genuine care, builds trust that transforms both individuals and organizations. Don't settle for surface-level leadership. Dive deeper. The most meaningful work happens below the waterline.

The question every leader must answer is this: Will you be a snorkeler or a scuba diver? Snorkelers stay safe on the surface, observing behaviors without ever understanding their origins, managing symptoms without addressing root causes. But scuba divers, the most effective leaders, are willing to go deep, to endure the pressure and discomfort that comes with exploring the glacier beneath, because they understand that lasting impact, genuine connection, and transformational leadership only happen when you're brave enough to leave the surface behind and dive into the depths where people actually live.

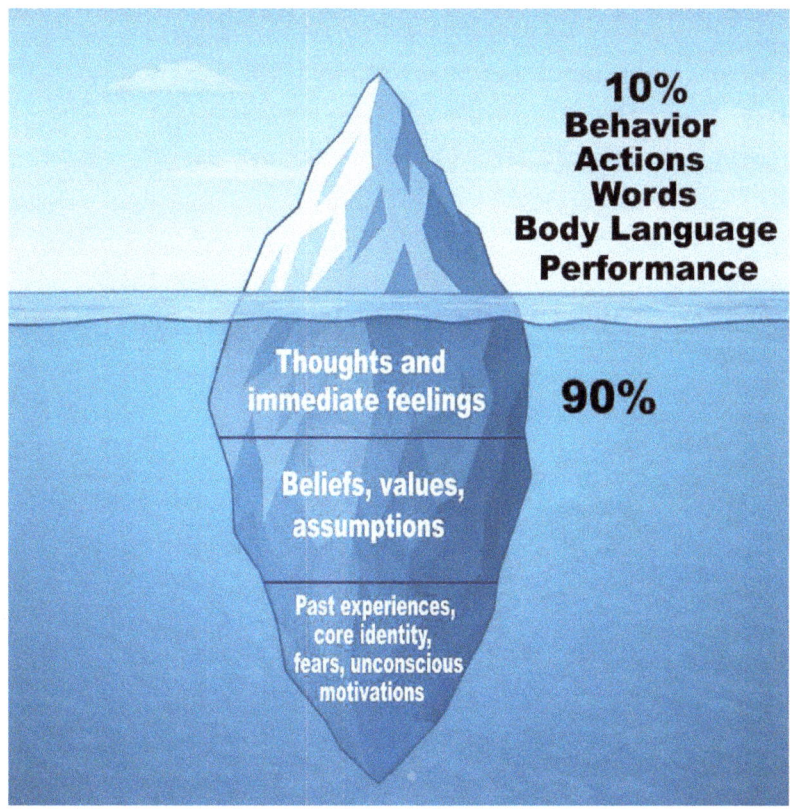

Chapter 22:

Conflict Management: A Core Competency

Elena, the senior manager, was reviewing the week's team reports with her supervisor, Greg, when she paused. "The marketing and sales teams barely speak to each other. I can feel the tension in joint meetings, but no one's saying anything directly. I'm not sure if I should address it or let them work it out."

Greg leaned back thoughtfully. "What do you think will happen if you wait?"

"It'll probably get worse," Elena admitted. "But I don't want to create drama where there isn't any."

"Here's what I've learned," Greg said. "Conflict doesn't disappear because we ignore it. It just goes underground and festers. You're thinking like a leader by recognizing that something is off. The question is: how can we create space for honest conversation before the resentment becomes irreparable? What if you brought both team leads together, named what you're observing without assigning blame, and asked them to help you understand what's happening?"

Elena nodded slowly. "So, address it early, but with curiosity, not judgment?"

"Exactly," Greg said. "Conflict is inevitable. Leadership is about how we respond to it. The fact that you're uncomfortable avoiding it tells me you're ready to lead through it. That instinct will serve you well."

Leadership Rule #108 - "Conflict is inevitable, how we deal with it is optional…"

Conflict is inevitable in any workplace, especially in environments rich with diverse perspectives and experiences. What distinguishes effective leaders is not the absence of conflict but their ability to navigate it with emotional intelligence. Our response, shaped by self-awareness, self-control, and empathy, determines whether conflict becomes a barrier or a bridge. Leaders who approach disagreements with respect and clarity foster collaboration, build trust, and turn tension into opportunity. While conflict is certain, choosing to handle it constructively is optional, and that choice begins with mastering communication and understanding others.

Conflict often triggers us because it touches deep layers of identity, values, and unresolved wounds. When our perspective is challenged, it can feel like a threat to belonging, activating old patterns rooted in past experiences. This reaction often drives us to defend rather than seek clarity because defense feels safer than vulnerability.

Leadership, however, calls for a heart posture that prioritizes understanding over winning.

Being "quick to listen and slow to speak" is more than a technique. It's an act of emotional intelligence requiring self-awareness and restraint. Pausing to recognize what's happening inside us before responding allows us to lead from strength rather than reactivity.

Before we explore how to manage conflict constructively, we must address one of the most insidious forms of workplace toxicity, like passive-aggressive behavior.

Unlike direct conflict, which at least brings issues to the surface for addressing, passive aggression operates in the shadows, undermining trust, eroding morale, and poisoning team dynamics without ever declaring itself openly. Passive-aggressive behavior is indirect resistance to expectations or requests, often accompanied by superficial compliance that masks underlying resentment, anger, or disagreement. In leadership contexts, it manifests in ways that are difficult to confront because they're designed to maintain plausible deniability. The leader says one thing, but their tone, body language, or subsequent actions communicate something entirely different. They agree to support a decision in the meeting but subtly sabotage it through delays, "forgetting" commitments, or making backhanded comments that undermine confidence.

Why is passive aggression so damaging? Because it operates below the surface, it is likened to that 90% of the iceberg we discussed in Chapter 21. Direct conflict can be addressed through the techniques we will explore in this chapter. But passive aggression is designed to evade accountability.

When confronted, the passive-aggressive person denies intent: "I didn't mean it that way." "You're being too sensitive." "I was just joking." The behavior continues; the pattern persists, and the team suffers, but there's never a clear moment of reckoning because the aggression is always veiled.

While passive-aggressive behavior manifests in many forms, strategic silence, backhanded compliance, and subtle sabotage, its most pervasive modern expression is email communication. Email provides the perfect conditions for passive-aggression to thrive. It serves as written documentation that can be defended as "professional," as asynchronous communication that avoids immediate confrontation, and as a means of copying others as witnesses without directly addressing the conflict.

And if you don't think this behavior is common: the average worker receives 121 emails per day, professionals spend 28% of their workday reading and responding to emails, 64% of employees have sent or received emails that caused unnecessary conflict, and poor email communication is cited as a top frustration in employee exit interviews.

Leaders who would never speak condescendingly face-to-face write emails dripping with barely concealed contempt. The phrases are familiar to anyone who's worked in an office.

What makes these phrases passive-aggressive isn't the literal words. It's the tone, timing, and context. "As per my last email" can serve as factual documentation when sent weeks later to someone who may have missed a message. But when sent the next day with a condescending edge, it's a public reprimand disguised as professionalism. The most insidious aspect? A passive-aggressive email often looks professional on the surface. It's polite. It uses complete sentences. It follows grammar rules. But underneath the veneer of professionalism is a weapon designed to undermine, embarrass, or assert dominance without direct confrontation.

Effective leaders recognize that how they communicate via email shapes team culture. If you model passive-aggression, your team will replicate it. If you model directness with respect, you create psychological safety. Email etiquette isn't culturally neutral. What reads as "direct and efficient" in low-context cultures (e.g., the U.S., Germany, the Netherlands) can feel abrupt or rude in high-context cultures (e.g., Japan, Korea, the Middle East, Latin America).

Leaders set the tone. If you model condescending, evasive, or publicly shaming communication, your team will replicate it. But if you model directness with respect, acknowledge mistakes gracefully, and handle conflict privately before escalating, you create a culture in which email becomes a tool for collaboration rather than a means of control.

Email should clarify, not confuse. It should document, not shame. It should connect, not divide. The helpful leader recognizes that every email is a choice: escalate or de-escalate, undermine or empower, hide or engage honestly.

Effective email communication requires intentional word choices that promote collaboration rather than condescension. Instead of writing "As per my last email…," which implies frustration and incompetence, use "Following up on my previous message...," which maintains respect while acknowledging the need for a response.

Replace "Just to be clear..." (which suggests the other person misunderstood) with "To make sure we're aligned..." (which assumes shared responsibility for clarity).

Rather than "Per my previous message..." (which sounds annoyed), try "Building on what I shared earlier..." (which frames the conversation as progressive).

Exchange "Please advise." (which distances you from problem-solving) for "What are your thoughts on next steps?" (which invites collaboration).

Swap "Going forward, let's make sure..." (which documents failure) with "For future reference, here's what works best..." (which offers guidance without blame).

Avoid CCing leadership on first follow-ups, which creates unnecessary pressure and public embarrassment; instead, have direct conversations first and escalate only if necessary. Finally, resist one-word replies when context is needed. Dismissive responses like "Noted" or "Fine" create confusion, and instead provide a clear acknowledgment, such as "Got it—I'll have this done by [time]. Thanks for the heads up." These small shifts in language transform email from a weapon of passive-aggression into a tool for respectful, productive communication.

The roots of passive aggression often lie in environments in which direct communication is punished or deemed unsafe. People who learned early in life, or in past work environments, that expressing disagreement led to retaliation, rejection, or being labeled "difficult" develop passive-aggressive patterns as survival mechanisms. They can't say no directly, so they say yes and then sabotage. They can't express anger openly, so they do so through withdrawal, sarcasm, or subtle noncompliance. The behavior isn't malicious. It's often a learned coping strategy, but that doesn't make it any less toxic. The solution is to develop emotional intelligence and the courage to communicate directly, even when it's uncomfortable. Say what you mean.

Mean what you say. If you disagree, say so. If you're hurt, name it.

Create a culture in which people feel safe to disagree openly, where "no" is an acceptable answer, and where direct communication is valued over superficial harmony. When people know they can express dissent without punishment, passive aggression loses its function.

Remember: passive aggression thrives in environments where people fear honesty. The antidote is psychological safety, which we've discussed throughout this book, and the modeling of direct, respectful communication, even (especially) when the message is difficult. Conflict managed openly can strengthen teams. Conflict hidden beneath passive-aggressive patterns destroys them slowly, quietly, and often irreparably.

Resolving conflict effectively also means considering what we know about the other person, their pressures, background, and even unspoken wounds. In helping professions, this is called seeing the whole person, and it applies equally to leadership. When we put others before ourselves, we create space for empathy and healing, transforming conflict into an opportunity for growth. This approach nurtures soul health, not only for those we lead but also for ourselves, by shifting the focus from self-protection to mutual understanding. Leaders who embrace this mindset of humility foster trust and turn tension into catalysts for deeper connection and collaboration.

When priorities clash, resources feel scarce, or objectives seem misaligned, conflict challenges a leader's ability to maintain cohesion. Leadership is not about avoiding tension but guiding it toward constructive outcomes. The responsibility lies in harmonizing competing interests so that decisions serve the greater good rather than narrow agendas. Effective leaders turn conflict into a catalyst for progress, sparking innovation, uncovering hidden issues, and deepening interdependence. Rather than viewing conflict as a threat, they frame it as an opportunity for clarity and growth.

Healthy tension, when managed well, strengthens teams and drives progress. Just as muscles require resistance to grow, organizations need constructive challenges to foster development and innovation. Without the tension, growth stalls, and potential remains untapped.

When conflict arises, especially when someone offends us, the following questions offer a powerful opportunity for self-reflection and inner exploration. Pastor Rich Villodas once said, *"A healthy soul pays attention to its reactions…"* **and suggested these five questions when processing our feelings:**

1. What happened?
2. What am I feeling?
3. What story am I telling myself?

4.   What do my values or beliefs tell me about the situation?

5.   What is the counterintuitive act required of me?

Pausing to reflect on these questions helps leaders move from reactive defensiveness to intentional clarity, fostering emotional intelligence and healthier relationships. A former colleague of mine, Wendy Whitlow, once said, *"You can disagree, but you don't have to be disagreeable."*

Many people avoid conflict because it feels uncomfortable, a form of self-preservation. We fear rejection, tension, or escalation, so we sidestep hard conversations rather than face them. Yet avoidance is often more damaging than not knowing how to resolve conflict; it allows misunderstandings to fester, erodes trust, and creates division. Emotional and spiritual health equips us to engage in conflict in ways that bring alignment rather than separation. This requires self-awareness, empathy, and courage to prioritize clarity over comfort. Leaders who embrace this posture model maturity and create space for growth, healing, and collaboration.

According to an article by Wi-Fi Talents titled "Workplace Conflict Statistics," nearly 45% of managers admit they avoid addressing conflicts directly, which often worsens the situation. Unresolved conflict costs U.S. businesses up to $359 billion annually in lost productivity, and organizations with high levels of unresolved conflict experience up to 11% higher turnover."

Avoidance doesn't eliminate conflict; it amplifies its impact. Leaders who develop emotional intelligence and soul health position themselves to transform these moments into opportunities for innovation, trust-building, and deeper connection.

Conflict theorists William Wilmot and Joyce Hocker once said, *"The basic choice in conflict is whether to avoid or engage, and engagement done well leads to transformation."*

Leadership Rule #151: "Clarity Heals, Defense Divides..."

When we're misunderstood or misrepresented, our instinct is to defend ourselves, to prove we're right, and protect our reputation.

However, this act is rooted in emotions such as hurt, offense, and a need for vindication.

It comes from a wounded place and often deepens conflict rather than resolving it.

Bringing clarity is different. It's rooted in the desire for unity and mutual understanding. Clarity isn't about winning; it's about creating shared truth, so both parties can move forward together. But you can't bring clarity while you're still wounded.

Before you can communicate clearly, you must first remove the emotional charge. This requires pausing, taking a breath, reflecting on what happened, processing your feelings with a mentor or counselor, and acting only then. When you approach the situation free from offense, your communication shifts. You're no longer reacting. But rather you're responding. You're no longer defending; you're clarifying.

The difference is profound. Defense says, "You're wrong about me." Clarity says, "Let me help us both see this more accurately." Defense escalates tension. Clarity dissolves it. Leaders who master this distinction transform conflict from a battleground into a bridge, one that strengthens trust, preserves relationships, and models emotional maturity.

Three Ways of Bringing Clarity:

1.   **Pause before responding** - Give yourself time to process emotions before engaging.

2.   **Seek understanding, not vindication** - Your goal is mutual clarity, not winning.

3.   **Communicate from a healed place** - Resolve your hurt privately so you can speak publicly with wisdom.

Leadership Rule #00: "Judge Methods, Not Motives..."

One of the most destructive habits in conflict is assuming we know why someone did what they did. We observe their methods, what they said, how they said it, the decision they made, and the action they took.

We immediately construct a narrative about their motives: "They did that because they don't respect me," "They're trying to undermine the team," "They're being selfish."

Here's the truth: You can observe and evaluate someone's methods, but you can never fully know their motives. Motives live beneath the surface, in the 90% of the iceberg we explored in Chapter 21. They're shaped by past experiences, unspoken fears, cultural conditioning, personal pressures, and internal narratives you'll never have complete access to. When you assume motives, you're filling gaps with your own projections, biases, and insecurities. This distinction is critical for effective conflict resolution.

When you judge methods, you can have a productive conversation: "When you sent that email without copying me, it created confusion for the client." That's observable, factual, and addressable.

But when you judge motives, you create defensiveness and escalation: "You deliberately excluded me because you don't value my input." Now you've made an accusation about their character and intent, which they'll almost certainly deny, and the conversation devolves into "Yes, you did." vs. "No, I didn't."

Consider this scenario: Your colleague misses a critical deadline, forcing you to scramble to cover their work.

You could assume their motive: "They're irresponsible and don't care about the team."

Or you could address the method: "The deadline was missed, which created problems. Help me understand what happened."

The first approach assumes intent and closes dialogue.

The second creates space for truth: "Maybe they were dealing with a family emergency, maybe they misunderstood the timeline, maybe they've been overwhelmed and afraid to ask for help."

You won't discover the real reason if you've already decided you know their motive. This doesn't mean you ignore the patterns. If someone repeatedly demonstrates methods that harm the team, chronic lateness, poor communication, failure to follow through, those patterns warrant direct conversation and accountability. But even then, you address observable behavior, not your assumptions about why they're doing it.

The principle of "judge methods, not motives" protects you from two dangers:

1. Prevents you from becoming the prosecutor in someone else's internal trial. When you assume negative motives, you've already convicted them in your mind before they have a chance to explain. This violates the psychological safety necessary for healthy teams.
2. Protects you from being wrong. How many times have you been certain someone intended harm, only to discover later they were completely

unaware of the impact? How many conflicts have escalated because both parties were responding to assumed motives rather than actual intent? Humility requires admitting that we don't have access to other people's inner worlds—we only see what they do, not why.

Next time you're in conflict, pause and separate these two questions:

1. "What did they do?" (Method - observable, factual)
2. "Why did they do it?" (Motive - assumption, interpretation)

Address question one directly. Explore question two with curiosity, not accusation: "Help me understand what was going on for you when you made that decision." This single shift, from judging motives to addressing methods, can transform how you navigate conflict, build trust, and preserve relationships even through difficult conversations. As we explored Chapter 6 on ego and humility, we found that the willingness to assume positive intent until proven otherwise is a mark of mature leadership. It doesn't make you naive; it makes you wise. Because the moment you start assigning motives, you can't verify; you've stopped leading and started projecting.

Chapter 23:

When Growth Isn't Possible, Graceful Exits

Leadership Rule #227 "Compassion and accountability aren't opposites, they are partners..."

Terminating an employee's employment is one of the most difficult responsibilities a leader faces. When poorly executed, it can devastate a person's confidence, damage their livelihood, and leave emotional scars that last a lifetime. Done well, it can preserve dignity, provide clarity, and even redirect someone toward a better fit. The difference isn't in the outcome; the person still loses their job, but in how their humanity is honored throughout the process.

If leadership is about cultivating people, what happens when someone can't thrive in the soil you've provided? What do you do when development efforts fail, when behavior violates non-negotiables, or when someone's presence actively harms the team they're meant to serve? The answer isn't to avoid accountability; it's to execute it with the same care, clarity, and respect you've shown throughout their tenure. Termination is not the opposite of helpful leadership; it's the most difficult expression of it.

Performance-based terminations stem from misalignment, not moral failure. When someone isn't succeeding in their role, helping them understand this isn't about their worth as a person. It's about them not being the right puzzle piece. Frame the conversation around the reality that this role or environment wasn't a good fit, and provide specific examples rather than vague statements like "you weren't meeting expectations." Where appropriate, provide support, such as references, networking connections, or resume assistance, to help them transition to opportunities better suited to their strengths.

Behavioral or ethical violations, however, require a different approach, one marked by firmness without cruelty. These conversations demand clarity about the connection between a person's actions and their consequences, leaving no ambiguity that could lead to rumors or speculation. While the termination is still delivered with respect for their humanity, the tone remains professional, and support beyond legal requirements may not be appropriate given the nature of the violation.

Before entering the conversation, ensure that your documentation is thorough and fair, and consult HR or legal counsel to protect both parties and maintain organizational integrity. Rehearse what you'll say. This isn't a conversation to improvise. Choose a private setting and an appropriate time; avoid Friday afternoons or other times that unnecessarily complicate matters. Have a clear plan for logistics, including the exit process, final paycheck, continuation of benefits, and the return of company property, so the person leaves with clarity about next steps rather than confusion about practicalities during an already overwhelming moment.

Termination requires holding two truths simultaneously: The integrity of the team is non-negotiable, and the dignity of the individual is sacred.

You can fire someone and still see them as a person made in the image of God (or however you frame human worth). You can uphold standards without dehumanizing those who don't meet them. You can protect your team from dysfunction without demonizing the person causing it.

If you lead long enough, you will fire someone. The question isn't whether you'll face this responsibility; it's whether you'll execute it in a way that protects your team's culture while honoring the person's humanity. Accountability and compassion aren't opposites; they're partners. The best leaders understand that the same hands that cultivate growth must sometimes prune with precision, and both require care, clarity, and a commitment to something larger than comfort.

Conclusion

Leadership in 2026 is the product of a century of change. The Silent Generation taught us the value of loyalty and stability. Baby Boomers reinforced the value of hard work and organizational commitment. Generation X challenged tradition, proving that adaptability and independence matter as much as tenure. Millennials redefined leadership as collaborative, purpose-driven, and transparent. Gen Z pushed us further, demanding authenticity, inclusivity, and social responsibility. And now, Gen Alpha signals a future where technology, personalization, and creativity will dominate the leadership landscape.

These shifts reveal a simple truth: Leadership is no longer about authority; it's about agility, empathy, and vision. Today's leaders must listen actively, communicate across platforms, and create environments where diverse perspectives thrive. They must balance structure with flexibility, provide growth opportunities for all, and lead with a purpose that resonates beyond profit.

Effective leadership is not confined to a title or position; it's rooted in mindset and character. According to Nitin Nohria, former Dean of Harvard Business School (2010-2020), character is something each of us must work to form and develop throughout our lives. Nohria also concluded that "some leaders fail to develop the ability to withstand the pressures of their positions. Instead of such pressures bringing out the best in them, they bring out their worst selves. The leaders then cave into these pressures, knowingly or unwittingly promoting wrongdoing in themselves or others, usually to achieve short-term gains."

Leadership begins with the willingness to influence positively, serve others, and align personal actions with organizational values. Even without formal authority, every individual leads in some capacity, whether guiding a team, supporting a colleague, or managing their own decisions. The essence of leadership lies in having the right heart for people, a genuine commitment to shared goals, and the investment in organizational success.

A helpful leader understands that leadership is not merely about managing tasks or assembling teams; it is about cultivating individuals' growth and creating an environment in which both individuals and the collective can thrive.

Whether in coaching, healthcare, law, or social work, the unifying principle is clear. True leadership requires balancing effective execution with genuine empathy.

Leaders who lean too heavily on relationships without accountability, or on tasks without care for people, fail to unlock their team's potential.

True leadership requires strength in both delivering results and nurturing the human spirit.

At the heart of this balance lies emotional intelligence and self-awareness. Helpful leaders are willing to "till the soil" of their own hearts by confronting biases, limitations, and areas for growth. They recognize that vulnerability through criticism or feedback is part of cultivating trust and resilience.

Behavioral science reinforces this truth: Psychological safety, empathy, and a growth mindset are essential for innovation and collaboration. By managing emotions, empathizing with others, and turning setbacks into opportunities, leaders model resilience and inspire those they guide. Such leaders embody stewardship, gratitude, conflict resolution skills, and effective communication.

Ultimately, the helpful leader executes effective leadership by embracing the help profession mindset we explored in the Introduction. Like counselors, coaches, and healthcare professionals, helpful leaders lead with empathy, problem-solving, and ethical responsibility, understanding that their influence extends far beyond immediate outcomes.

Here is the paradox that every helpful leader encounters: The greatest reward for this approach isn't found in titles earned, promotions received, or accolades accumulated. It's found in the profound satisfaction of witnessing transformation in the people you've invested in. When the team member you coached through failure becomes confident. When the employee you believed in, when no one else did, got promoted. When someone you mentored three years ago reaches out to tell you how a conversation you barely remember changed the trajectory of their career. When you see someone leading their own team with the same servant-hearted posture you displayed, these moments, quiet, often private, rarely celebrated publicly, are the currency that helpful leaders value most.

This is leadership that transcends quarterly reviews and performance metrics. It's leadership that shows up in wedding invitations from team members who want you there because you cared about their whole life, not just their productivity. It shows up in LinkedIn messages from people who left your organization years ago but still credit you as the leader who changed how they see themselves. It shows up in the middle of difficult days when you're questioning whether any of this matters, and someone on your team pulls you aside to say, "I just want you to know, working for you has made me a better person, not just a better employee."

That's the reward. Not the corner office. Not the bigger budget. Not even recognition from senior leadership, though that may come. The reward is knowing that your leadership created space for people to become more themselves, to discover capacities they didn't know they had, to heal from wounds inflicted by past leaders, and to carry forward a vision of leadership that prioritizes human dignity alongside organizational excellence. You can't quantify that impact. You can't put it on a resume. But you can feel it, in the relationships that endure long after reporting structures to change, in the leaders you've helped shape who are now shaping others, in the quiet knowledge that you used your influence to leave people better than you found them.

Effective leaders empower dreamers to soar, channel creativity into practical results, and recognize that every interaction is an opportunity to make a lasting impact on someone's life. By investing in people, pruning distractions, fertilizing minds with knowledge, and watering spirits with purpose, they create ecosystems of trust, resilience, and innovation.

Their greatest contribution is not self-advancement but raising others up to yield a harvest of impact and influence that transforms organizations and communities alike. **And in doing so, they prove what I've witnessed throughout my career:** Leadership transcends culture, language, and industry when it's rooted in seeing people, valuing people, and supporting people to become everything they were created to be.

Bonus Chapter:

The H.E.L.P. Wheel

If you've made it to this section, I just want to say thank you! Former basketball coach John Wooden once said, *"The mind is the leader of your soul, so it has to be led by something."*

To complement the insights provided, I'd like to share a strategy to help you execute any of the ideas mentioned above. Introduced to me by my Pastor, Michael Cruz, the H.E.L.P. Wheel (also known as the Health-Empowered Life Plan) is a tool to help you see yourself as you were created to be.

Each part of the wheel represents an area of our lives: Mental, Emotional, Physical, Communal, and Spiritual Health. When one area is weak or neglected, the whole wheel struggles to roll smoothly. When each area is strengthened, your life moves forward with peace, purpose, and joy.

Observe each quadrant of the wheel and ask yourself the following questions:

1.   **Mental (your mind)** - Are my thoughts leading me closer to the reason for which I was created, or keeping me stuck?

- Your thoughts shape your reality. A renewed mind leads to hope, resilience, and a clear purpose, whereas a troubled mind keeps one stuck in fear and defeat.

2. **Emotional (your heart)** - Am I managing my emotions in healthy ways or reacting based on inner wounds?

- Unhealed emotions create cycles of anger, anxiety, and broken relationships. Emotional health brings freedom, peace, and the ability to love/serve others well.

3. **Physical (your body)** - Am I caring for my body with rest, nutrition, and energy to carry out purposeful living?

- Your body is the vehicle with which you can carry out your purpose on earth. When it's weak, sick, or exhausted, everything else suffers. Health is the energy that moves your life forward.

4. **Communal (your relationships)** - Am I connected to healthy, purpose-filled relationships or isolated from those around me?

- Isolation leads to stagnation. We were created for connection, to grow with and through others. A healthy community brings accountability, encouragement, and shared strength.

5. **Spiritual (the hub/axle connection)** - Is my relationship with my Creator thriving, or do I feel distant and dry?

• Without a strong center, the wheel falls off. Spiritual health keeps everything aligned, giving you direction, strength, and hope…no matter what road you are on.

• When your spirit is whole, the journey has a purpose. Without it, even success can feel empty.

As you reflect on these questions, evaluate each section of the wheel and assign a score from 1 to 10, where 1 indicates significant struggle and 10 represents thriving. Shade each quadrant from the center outward to visualize your rating. A fully shaded quadrant reflects strength in that area, while minimal shading highlights areas that may require focused attention and improvement.

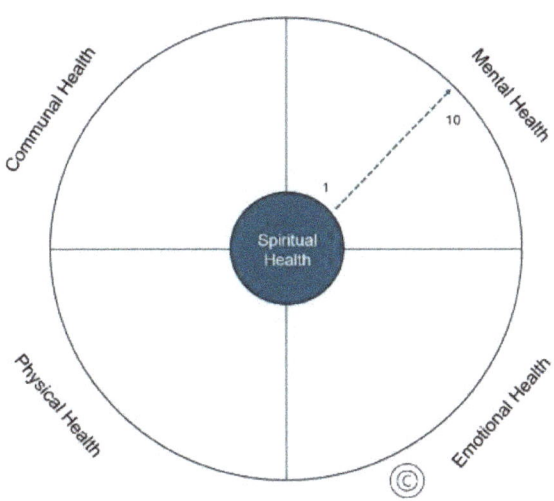

Throughout our time together, we've explored leadership as a holistic practice, one that begins with self-awareness and extends to how we influence others. The H.E.L.P. Wheel reinforces this truth by reminding us that leadership effectiveness is rooted in personal health across every dimension of life. Just as emotional intelligence and communication shape our ability to lead, maintaining balance across mental, emotional, physical, communal, and spiritual health ensures we lead from strength rather than depletion.

By integrating these principles, we move beyond theory to practical alignment: when the leader is whole, the impact on people and organizational success becomes transformational.

Appendix A:

Cross-Cultural Leadership Field Guide

When Entering a New Cultural Context, Ask:

About Respect:

- How is respect shown here? (Titles? Bowing? Eye contact? Elders first?)

- What behaviors signal disrespect, even unintentionally?

About Communication:

- Is directness valued or offensive?

- How is disagreement expressed appropriately?

- What does silence mean in this culture?

About Decision-Making:

- Are decisions made individually or collectively?

- Who needs to be consulted before decisions are final?

- How long does consensus-building typically take?

About Time:

- What does "on time" mean here?

- Is punctuality respect or is flexibility relationship-honoring?

- How are deadlines communicated and negotiated?

About Relationships:

- Must trust be built before business, or can they develop simultaneously?

- What builds trust in this context?

- How much personal sharing is appropriate professionally?

About Hierarchy:

- How is authority expressed and challenged?

- Can I be questioned by subordinates? Should I invite it?

- What creates or destroys credibility here?

About Feedback:

- How is constructive criticism given without offense?

- Public or private? Direct or indirect?

- Who can give feedback to whom?

About Work-Life Integration:

- Are family obligations respected as legitimate work considerations?

- Are after-hours social events expected? Optional? Inappropriate?

- How are religious observances honored?

Common Cross-Cultural Mistakes and How to Recover:

Mistake: Using first names too quickly in a hierarchical culture

- **Recovery:** "I apologize, in my culture we use first names quickly, but I want to show proper respect. Please tell me how you'd prefer to be addressed."

Mistake: Being too direct in a high-context culture

- **Recovery:** "I realize I may have been too blunt. In my culture, directness shows respect, but I'm learning different approaches. Can we discuss this again?"

Mistake: Misinterpreting silence as agreement

- **Recovery:** "I want to make sure I'm understanding correctly. When I asked for concerns and heard silence, did that mean agreement, or was there something you preferred to discuss privately?"

Mistake: Scheduling meetings during prayer time/religious observance

- **Recovery:** "I apologize for not accounting for [prayer time/Ramadan/festival]. Help me understand the schedule I should work around so I can be more respectful going forward."

Showing Respect: Practical Phrases

In many cultures, respect is demonstrated through specific linguistic practices, honorific titles, formal greetings, or phrases that acknowledge relationships before business. Learning and using these culturally appropriate expressions signals that you value the person and their cultural norms, building trust before any work discussion begins.

Below are a few examples of showing respect in this way:

- **Japan/Korea:** Use family name + "-san" (Mr./Ms.) until explicitly told otherwise: "Tanaka-san, may I ask your opinion?"

- **Arabic-speaking regions:** Begin meetings with "As-salamu alaykum" (peace be upon you) rather than jumping straight to business

- **Latin America:** "¿Cómo está su familia?" (How is your family?) before discussing work shows genuine care.

- **India:** Adding "-ji" as a suffix shows respect: "Sharma-ji, thank you for your guidance."

- **South Africa (Zulu):** "Sawubona" (I see you) - literal translation reveals cultural value of being truly seen.

The Universal Principles: Across every culture, these remain true:

- People want to be seen, valued, and respected

- Trust is built through consistency and integrity

- Growth happens when people feel psychologically safe

- Purpose motivates more than fear

- Relationships are the foundation of influence

The methods adapt. The principles endure.

Appendix B: The Measurable Impact of Emotional Intelligence

The following research demonstrates how emotional intelligence directly impacts organizational performance and profitability. This data, compiled from multiple sources by the Consortium for Research on Emotional Intelligence in Organizations, provides practitioners and managers with evidence-based tools to strengthen their leadership capabilities.

Financial Performance: The U.S. Air Force implemented emotional intelligence assessments for recruiter selection and saved $3 million annually by increasing their ability to predict successful recruiters nearly threefold.

Productivity and Safety: After manufacturing supervisors received training in emotional competencies such as active listening and collaborative problem-solving, lost-time accidents decreased by 50%, formal grievances dropped from 15 per year to 3, and the plant exceeded productivity goals by $250,000. At another facility with similar training, production increased by 17%—with no corresponding increase at plants where supervisors weren't trained.

Leadership Effectiveness: Research analyzing more than 300 top executives across 15 global companies identified six emotional competencies that distinguished exceptional leaders from average leaders: influence, team leadership, organizational awareness, self-confidence, achievement drive, and leadership capability. A study of 515 senior executives across Latin America, Germany, and Japan found that emotional intelligence was a better predictor of success than either relevant experience or IQ, with high EI present in 74% of successful executives but only 24% of failures.

These aren't isolated findings. Competency research across more than 200 organizations worldwide suggests that approximately one-third of performance differences stem from technical skills and cognitive abilities, whereas two-thirds stem from emotional competence. In top leadership positions, more than four-fifths of the performance difference is attributable to emotional competence.

The implications are clear: organizations that invest in developing emotional intelligence—through better selection processes, targeted training, and leadership development— see measurable returns in profitability, retention, productivity, and leadership effectiveness. This isn't about making people "feel good." It's about driving organizational performance through human capability.

These findings are drawn from research conducted by the Consortium for Research on Emotional Intelligence in Organizations, compiled by Dr. Cary Cherniss at Rutgers University. Full citations are available in the references section.

In Their Own Words (cont'd)

"James has not only been pivotal to the success of our Quality and Regulatory divisions, but also an outstanding employee development ambassador at Centerfield Media. He contributed unquantifiable value towards employees' professional development and executed methodologies that counteracted the loss of revenue. As his subordinate, James demonstrated leadership qualities consistently and applied a mentorship dynamic, which led him to establish a well-respected Quality team. He knows the true essence of professionalism and commitment. As he escalated ranks due to his proven qualities and success in his prior role, he acquired the Sr. Director of Training position, which consequently paved the way for me to become his successor. In this position, he exhibited once again his "we're in this together" attitude and rolled up his sleeves to revamp the training wing.

With close off/on-site presence, he earned the trust and respect of his new team and remained collaborative with our Quality team. Under that role, he demonstrated his ability to overcome cultural lifestyle differences (Caribbean vs. U.S.) and launched professional growth seminars that sparked positive feedback throughout all of our locations."

- Dayana P. Ramos, Quality Assurance/Customer Analytics, EarthLink Internet

"James Oyola created an environment where trust and empowerment weren't just encouraged—they were the foundation. He gave us the freedom to make decisions, contribute ideas, and take ownership of our work. His leadership style built confidence across the team, and the respect and openness he showed allowed us to thrive. It's rare to find leaders who genuinely empower their teams the way he did."

- Princess Nieves, 20 years in administrative work, sales, and customer service

"James Oyola has been one of the most impactful leaders of my career. He didn't just recognize my potential for leadership—he actively invested in it. James was intentional about developing people, and in my case, he thoughtfully created a leadership progression path that equipped me with real, transferable skills I continue to use to this day. What set James apart was his ability to both challenge and advocate for his team. He pushed me beyond my comfort zone while also providing the structure, trust, and guidance needed to succeed.

Because of his leadership, I gained confidence in my ability to lead, influence, and make strategic decisions—foundations that continue to shape my career. Being led by James meant being seen not just for where you were, but for where you could go—and having a leader willing to help you get there."

- Chelsea Eyma, 15 years in sales and customer service

"James, I think this year has been so much better than the last. I have grown a lot since you joined the account, and I appreciate you a lot for that. Before I took the job at Global, I was interviewing at other places, and some of the interview questions were about things I have done to further myself, things that have challenged me. This was hard for me to answer. After years and years of being a lead with no new goals or growth training, I didn't have much to say. But I feel like I have grown so much just from learning how to adapt to having a split team, new personalities, new goals, etc. I have done so many new things, and I feel a lot more confident in my abilities."

- Krystal Phillips, Supervisor, The Company Store

"After today's session with James and my other colleagues, I felt that it was time for me to start working on things that I knew within myself I had to improve. The last session was more personal for me and has put into perspective things I have to discuss with my family and put an end to."

-   Anonymous, Leadership Workship Review

"Dear James, thank you for being such a wonderful boss. You know how to bring out the best in your employees. Please accept my heartfelt appreciation for all of the support and motivation! You are so helpful, kind, and generous with your time and energy. Thank you so much for being an excellent manager! Your leadership skills make it easy for you to manage our team, even with our diverse professional backgrounds. I'm proud to have learned some of these qualities from you. Thank you for guiding me professionally and personally."

- Yanique Grazzal, 10 years in sales and customer service

References

Adobe. (2019). 2019 U.S. emoji trend report. https://www.adobe.com/express/learn/blog/emoji-trend-report

A. Mehrabian, Silent Messages (Belmont, CA: Wadsworth, 1981)

American Psychological Association. (2021). Work and well-being survey. https://www.apa.org/pubs/reports/work-well-being

American Psychological Association. (2023). 2023 Work in America Survey: Workplaces as engines of psychological health and well-being. https://www.apa.org/pubs/reports/work-in-america/2023-workplace-health-well-being

Autry, J. A. (2001). The servant leader: How to build a creative team, develop great morale, and improve bottom-line performance. Crown Business.

Bachman, J., Stein, S., Campbell, K., & Sitarenios, G. (2000). Emotional intelligence in the collection of debt. International Journal of Selection and Assessment, 8(3), 176-182.

Boyatzis, R. (1982). The competent manager: A model for effective performance. John Wiley and Sons.

Boyatzis, R. E. (1999, September 27). From a presentation to the Linkage Conference on Emotional Intelligence [Conference presentation]. Chicago, IL.

Brown, S. (2009). Play: How it shapes the brain, opens the imagination, and invigorates the soul. W.W. Norton.

Burke, T. (2020). Empathy. Rider.

Burning for Success. (n.d.). Ego quotes. Retrieved December 19, 2025, from https://burningforsuccess.com/ego-quotes/

Business Insider. (2016, June 7). Why you should greet your co-workers every day. Inc.com. https://www.inc.com/business-insider/why-you-should-greet-your-co-workers-everyday.html

Cherniss, C. (n.d.). Consortium for Research on Emotional Intelligence in Organizations. Rutgers University. Retrieved December 19, 2025, from http://www.eiconsortium.org

Chief Talent Officer. (2025, April 7). The hidden costs of leadership cultures: Moving from leader-centric to team-focused. https://www.chieftalentofficer.co/2025/04/07/the-hidden-costs-of-leadership-cultures-moving-from-leader-centric-to-team-focused/

Crum, T. (n.d.). The quality of our lives depends not on whether or not we have conflicts, but on how we respond to them. In Conflict Resolution Quotes. Global Peace Careers. Retrieved December 19, 2025, from https://globalpeacecareers.com/magazine/conflict-resolution-quotes/

Forbes Technology Council. (2024, September 20). Using values-based hiring to attract and retain mission-driven employees. Forbes. https://www.forbes.com/councils/forbestechcouncil/2024/09/20/using-values-based-hiring-to-attract-and-retain-mission-driven-employees/

Gallup. (2015). State of the American Manager Report. https://www.gallup.com/services/182138/state-american-manager-report.aspx

Gallup. (n.d.). Employee engagement on the rise in the U.S. Retrieved December 19, 2025, from https://news.gallup.com/poll/241649/employee-engagement-rise.aspx

George, B., Sims, P., McLean, A. N., & Mayer, D. (2007). Managing authenticity: The paradox of great leadership. Harvard Business Review, 85(2), 129–138.

Gittell, J. H. (2003). The Southwest Airlines way: Using the power of relationships to achieve high performance. McGraw-Hill.

Goleman, D. (1995). Emotional intelligence: Why it can matter more than IQ. Bantam Books.

Goleman, D. (1998). Working with emotional intelligence. Bantam Books.

Goodreads. (n.d.). Conflict quotes. Retrieved December 19, 2025, from https://www.goodreads.com/quotes/tag/conflict

Grammarly & The Harris Poll. (2022). The state of business communication.
https://www.grammarly.com/business/learn/business-communication-statistics/

Grant, A. (2021, April 13). The science of productive conflict [Audio podcast transcript]. WorkLife with Adam Grant. TED. https://www.ted.com/podcasts/worklife/the-science-of-productive-conflict-transcript

Hay Group. (2013). Seven steps to measure and build engagement the right way. Enterprise Engagement Alliance. https://www.enterpriseengagement.org/direct/user/site/1/files/Seven-Steps-to-Measure-and-Build-Engagement-the-Right-Way-Hay-Group-full-report.pdf

Hay/McBer Research and Innovation Group. (1997). [Research data provided to Daniel Goleman]. In D. Goleman, Working with emotional intelligence. Bantam Books.

HBR Editors. (2025, September). The secret to building a high-performing team. Harvard Business Review. https://hbr.org/2025/09/the-secret-to-building-a-high-performing-team

High5. (2023). Communication in the workplace statistics. https://high5test.com/communication-in-the-workplace-statistics/

Holmes, M. (2011). The cost of poor communications. The Holmes Report.

HR Leader. (2025, April 7). Is saying good morning to a colleague a dying interaction? https://www.hrleader.com.au/wellbeing/25383-is-saying-good-morning-to-a-colleague-a-dying-interaction

Hunter, J. E., Schmidt, F. L., & Judiesch, M. K. (1990). Individual differences in output variability as a function of job complexity. Journal of Applied Psychology, 75, 28-42.

Hurt, K., & Dye, D. (2016). Winning well: A manager's guide to getting results—without losing your soul. AMACOM.

Ideawake. (n.d.). The success of Toyota's employee suggestion program. Retrieved December 19, 2025, from https://ideawake.com/the-success-of-toyotas-employee-suggestion-program/

Lebrecht, N. (2010). Why Mahler? How one man and ten symphonies changed our world. Anchor Books.

Lusch, R. F., & Serpkeuci, R. (1990). Personal differences, job tension, job outcomes, and store performance: A study of retail managers. Journal of Marketing.

Maccoby, M. (2004, January). Narcissistic leaders: The incredible pros, the inevitable cons. Harvard Business Review. https://hbr.org/2004/01/narcissistic-leaders-the-incredible-pros-the-inevitable-cons

Mandela, N. (1999). Long walk to freedom. Penguin.

Maslow, A. H. (1970). Motivation and personality (2nd ed.). Harper & Row.

McClelland, D. C. (1999). Identifying competencies with behavioral-event interviews. Psychological Science, 9(5), 331-339.

McKinsey Global Institute. (2012). The social economy: Unlocking value and productivity through social technologies. McKinsey & Company.

McKinsey & Company. (2015). Building organizational capabilities: McKinsey case study on leadership culture. https://www.mckinsey.com

Microsoft. (2021). The next great disruption is hybrid work—Are we ready? Work Trend Index. https://www.microsoft.com/en-us/worklab/work-trend-index

Nedergaard, M., & Goldman, S. A. (2020). Glymphatic failure as a final common pathway to dementia. Science, 370(6512), 50-56. https://doi.org/10.1126/science.abb8739

New York Times. (n.d.). Q&A with Nitin Nohria. Retrieved December 19, 2025, from https://www.nytimes.com

Penn State Leadership Blog. (2020, April 6). Southwest Airlines servant leadership creates organizational success. https://sites.psu.edu/leadership/2020/04/06/southwest-airlines-servant-leadership-creates-organizational-success/

Pesuric, A., & Byham, W. (1996, July). The new look in behavior modeling. Training and Development, 25-33.

Pontefract, D. (2020, August 4). Purpose-driven companies outperform the financial markets by 42 percent. https://www.danpontefract.com/purpose-driven-companies-outperform-the-financial-markets-by-42-percent/

Porkka-Heiskanen, T., Strecker, R. E., & McCarley, R. W. (2000). Brain site-specificity of extracellular adenosine concentration changes during sleep deprivation and spontaneous sleep. Neuroscience, 99(3), 507-517.

Porras, J. I., & Anderson, B. (1981). Improving managerial effectiveness through modeling-based training. Organizational Dynamics, 9, 60-77.

QuoteMaster. (n.d.). Conflict theory quotes. Retrieved December 19, 2025, from https://www.quotemaster.org/conflict+theory

Radicati Group. (2021). Email statistics report, 2021-2025. https://www.radicati.com/wp/wp-content/uploads/2021/Email-Statistics-Report-2021-2025-Executive-Summary.pdf

Ribeiro, J. A., & Sebastião, A. M. (2010). Caffeine and adenosine. Journal of Alzheimer's Disease, 20(s1), S3-S15.

Richman, L. S. (1994, May 16). How to get ahead in America. Fortune, 46-54.

Sandberg, S. (2020). Leadership is about making others better as a result of your presence and making sure that impact lasts in your absence. In A. Smith & B. Johnson

(Eds.), Leadership: The art of making others better (pp. 123-130). ABC Company.

Scazzero, P. (2015). The emotionally healthy leader: How transforming your inner life will deeply transform your church, team, and the world. Zondervan.

Schock, N. (2025, March 14). The one question that created Southwest Airlines' culture. https://nathanschock.com/2025/03/14/the-one-question-that-created-southwest-airlines-culture/

Seligman, M. E. P. (1990). Learned optimism. Knopf.

Sendmail, Inc. (2019). The impact of email in the workplace.

Shanafelt, T. D., Boone, S., Tan, L., Dyrbye, L. N., Sotile, W., Satele, D., Sloan, J., & Oreskovich, M. R. (2012). Burnout and satisfaction with work-life balance among US physicians relative to the general US population. Mayo Clinic Proceedings, 87(11), 1293-1300. https://www.mayoclinicproceedings.org/article/S0025-6196%2813%2900889-6/fulltext

Slack Technologies. (2023). State of work report. https://slack.com/blog/news/the-state-of-work-2023

Spencer, L. M., Jr., & Spencer, S. (1993). Competence at work: Models for superior performance. John Wiley and Sons.

Spencer, L. M., Jr., McClelland, D. C., & Kelner, S. (1997). Competency assessment methods: History and state of the art. Hay/McBer.

The Home Depot. (2024). 2024 annual report and proxy statement. https://ir.homedepot.com/~/media/Files/H/HomeDepot-IR/reports-and-presentations/annual-reports/2024-annual-report.pdf

The Interview Guys. (2025). Workplace burnout in 2025: Research report. https://blog.theinterviewguys.com/workplace-burnout-in-2025-research-report/

Towers Watson. (2014). Change and communication ROI study report 2013–2014.

Tupper, H., & Ellis, S. (2022, July 4). It's time to reimagine employee retention. Harvard Business Review. https://hbr.org/2022/07/its-time-to-reimagine-employee-retention

Viola, F. (2008). From eternity to here: Rediscovering the ageless purpose of God. David C Cook.

Visier. (2025). Employee productivity: Definition and tips. https://www.visier.com/blog/employee-productivity/

Walter V. Clarke Associates. (1996). Activity vector analysis: Some applications to the concept of emotional intelligence. Author.

WifiTalents Team. (2025, June 2). Workplace conflict statistics. WifiTalents. https://wifitalents.com/workplace-conflict-statistics/

Wilmot, W. W., & Hocker, J. L. (2017). Interpersonal conflict (10th ed.). McGraw-Hill Education.

Wooden, J., & Jamison, S. (1997). Wooden: A lifetime of observations and reflections on and off the court. McGraw-Hill.

Xie, L., Kang, H., Xu, Q., Chen, M. J., Liao, Y., Thiyagarajan, M., ... & Nedergaard, M. (2013). Sleep drives metabolite clearance from the adult brain. Science, 342(6156), 373-377. https://doi.org/10.1126/science.1241224

www.ingramcontent.com/pod-product-compliance
Lightning Source LLC
Chambersburg PA
CBHW051512120626
46551CB00012B/894